ESCAPE FROM LAOS

DIETER DENGLER

PRESIDIO

Copyright © 1979 by Presidio Press

Published by Presidio Press
505 B San Marin Drive, Suite 300
Novato, CA 94945-1340

This edition printed 1996

All rights reserved. No part of this book may be reproduced or utilized in any form or by any means, electronic or mechanical, including photocopying, recording, or by any information storage and retrieval systems, without permission in writing from the publisher. Inquiries should be addressed to Presidio Press, 505 B San Marin Drive, Suite 300, Novato, CA 94945-1340.

Library of Congress-in-Publication Data

Dengler, Dieter.
  Escape from Laos.
  1. Vietnamese Conflict, 1961–1975—Prisoners and prisons, Lao. 2. Dengler, Dieter. 3. Prisoners of war—United States—Biography. 4. Prisoners of war—Laos—Biography. I. Title.
DS559.4.D44   959.704'37 [B]   78-32056
ISBN: 0-89141-293-X

Printed in the United States of America

To Eugene Deatrick, the man who saved my life; to William E. Cowell and his helicopter crew; to Dr. Allan Holmes; and to all the others too numerous to mention who were so kind.

CONTENTS

Prologue, *1*

1 Crash, *7*

2 Capture, *15*

3 March, *27*

4 Interrogation, *55*

5 First Flight, *65*

6 End of the Line, *79*

7 Par Kung: Prison Camp, *91*

8 Hoi Het: New Home, *113*

9 Final Plans, *135*

10 Escape, *147*

11 Jungle Nightmare, *163*

12 Rescue, *187*

Epilogue, *205*

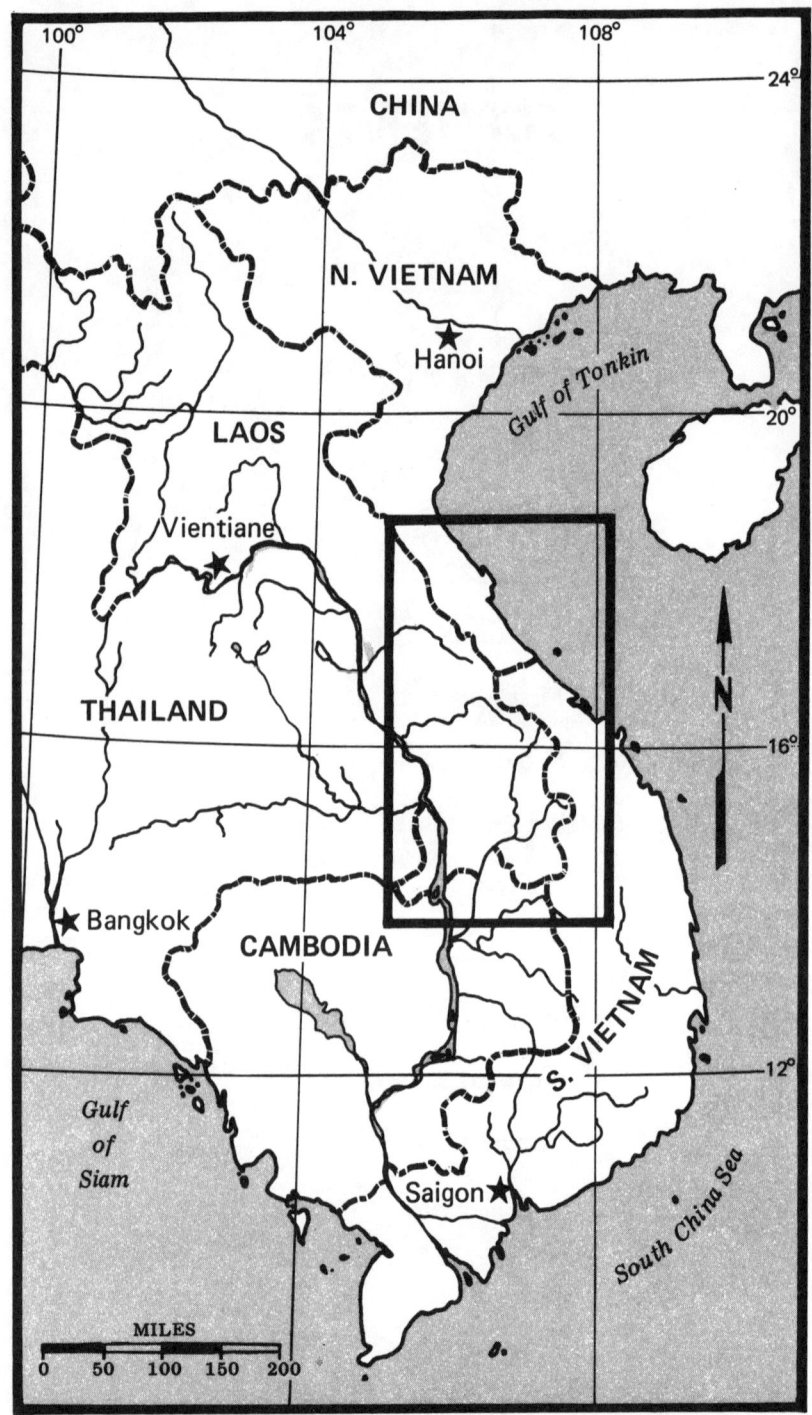

Southeast Asia. Enlargement of insert opposite.

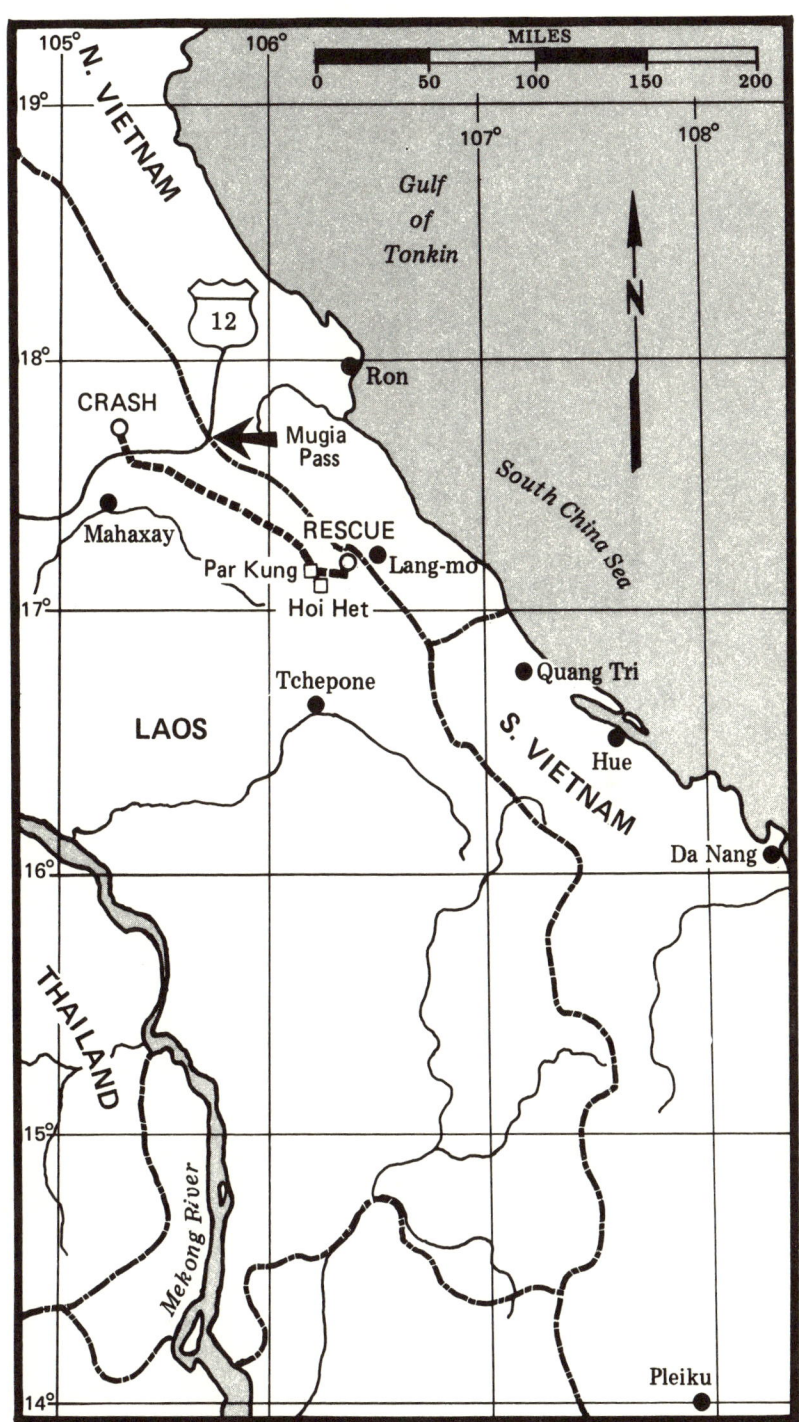

Specific area of crash and escape.

PROLOGUE

Late on the night of January 31, 1966, the duty officer of Attack Squadron VA-145 received word that our aircraft carrier was on its way from Dixie Station, just off the coast of South Vietnam, to the new station up north, the Gulf of Tonkin. All pilots were busy getting the latest information on roads, known missile sites, and whatever else they could lay their hands on. Air Intelligence, deep inside the carrier, was jammed with pilots, many wearing their dark brown flying jackets. One could see by the unshaven faces that they had been there a long time.

North Vietnam had not been bombed at all during the entire month of January, following the de-escalation policy. Therefore, it was not hard to guess that the Vietnamese had relocated every antiaircraft gun, missile site, and supply route during such an ideal bombing lull. We would have to fly our sorties without knowing where to expect to be singled out by a foreign-made, radar-controlled trap. It was hardly a thrilling thought.

We were supposed to have stayed at Dixie for at least one month. There I had flown a few easy carrier missions with little opposition from antiaircraft guns, a good way to get broken in on my first tour of duty in the Orient. Now, after only sixteen days, Washington decided to send us north to Yankee Station off the coast of North Vietnam. We pilots did not greet this news with joy and laughter because it meant an end to easy missions and the beginning of the rough stuff.

That night of January 31 seemed endless. All of us went painstakingly over our briefings on survival tactics, and I am sure every pilot contemplated, as I did, what he would do if he were shot down. In fact, I had begun thinking about it at least six months prior to our departure from Alameda Naval Air Station on the carrier U.S.S. *Ranger*, bound for the South China Sea. That was December 1965. I was no more worried about being shot down than the other pilots of my squadron, but I had a keener appreciation of the problems of survival because my early life had been so different from most of theirs.

I was born in 1938 in the small Black Forest village of Wildberg in southern Germany. It was a very peaceful town nestled between rolling green farmlands broken by fir trees and farm sheds. Even when the war began, nothing changed. Occasionally some planes would fly over, Allied or German, but no one worried about them. High up on the windy ridge above our town the Hitler Youth kept some gliders used for training young boys to fly. It was hoped the gliders would spark interest in flying and motivate young men to enlist in the Luftwaffe.

In 1944 a sudden change came to the peaceful village and we became very conscious of the war. My mother received word that my father had been killed in Russia. Soon after, Wildberg received its first visit from Allied fighter planes. They came screaming down the streets, only a few feet above the ground, lower than the upper window of our two-story house. The fighter planes flew so close that I could easily see the pilots. I remember one of them in particular, strapped in the cockpit, flashing by at about thirty feet from our front window. I remember his large black goggles and his machine that spat staccato yellow flashes.

The railway workers had pushed the old steam locomotives out onto the tracks, while the newer ones were safe, deep inside the tunnel. The American fighters were now making low passes to strafe them, pulling out in steep, right climbing turns to avoid the ridge beyond.

Perhaps because the planes were only after the trains and because the raids became such a regular occurrence, we children now regarded the raids as play. They lasted only a few minutes and when they were over the tougher boys ran across the tracks, looking for bullets. Some of them were lucky enough to find an entire cartridge belt to wear proudly. At that time I would never have understood nor anticipated that someday I, as a pilot, would spread the same kind of fear among peasants in a land thousands of miles away. I was captivated by those sleek-looking planes with loud screaming engines and I could not imagine anything in the world more exciting than to fly one of them.

Our games soon ended. One day the air raid sirens sounded. My mother hurried my brothers and me out the door. We ran through the village, up the dirt road toward the glider field for about two hundred yards, and then took a narrow winding path into the woods. There were a few shelters in our town, but nobody used them and the woods were by far the safest place to be.

We had just reached the first trees when the drone of large bomber airplanes reached us. Instead of flying right over our town as usual, the planes turned, circled, and let go of their great loads. I had never before heard the nerve-racking, whistling sound of bombs, nor the deafening booms from their explosions. The ground erupted, and within minutes our town was aflame. The bombers vanished as fast as they had come. Covered with leaves, I hugged the ground, pressing my hands over my ears long after the planes had finished their job. Cautiously we left the woods, looking down toward Wildberg. Everything seemed to be gone—utterly destroyed. As we walked back into town, we saw that most of the dead and wounded had already been lined up in rows. Horses and cows lay on their sides, their bellies ripped open by the blasts.

We were surprised to find our house still in a somewhat upright position, since three bombs had landed next to it, two on the right and one on the left. They must have gone off simultaneously, squeezing the house together but not toppling it. We were luckier than most of the people, who lost everything. As we came nearer, we saw that the kitchen side of our house was completely exposed, with the stucco walls blown away and part of the tile roof lying across the street. Inside we found piano keys and spoons with names engraved on them, from houses blocks away. It was a miracle that our house had not burned, because white-hot bomb splinters had ripped through everything, torn through the closets, and singed fist-sized holes in our clothing. With tears in her eyes, my mother salvaged the remains of our possessions to the sidewalk, knowing that the house would soon collapse.

I was only five years old then. Our home was gone and there was no place for us to stay in Wildberg. We packed what little we had and traveled aboard a smoking old truck that had been converted for burning wood chips, to my grandparents' house in Calw, about twenty-five kilometers away. My grandfather had a bakery, which was fortunate since food was so scarce, especially once the war was over and Calw was occupied by the French Moroccans.

The Moroccans arrived like a conquering army. I was standing in the bakery, hanging onto my mother's skirt, when they entered the house. Wide-eyed and scared, I stared at those men who were a different color from me. Three burst into our bakery and with axes smashed open closets. As soon as they left, Grandfather hurried us into the deep cellar where he stored his hard cider and potatoes. We sat on apple crates stacked against the rocky walls, and the total silence was broken only by an occasional drop of water falling from the curved ceiling. The only light was a candle set atop a cider barrel. Suddenly, the cellar door was kicked open and the candle knocked over. A small red light danced back and forth, coming closer and closer until it was held only inches from my face. The Moroccans hauled away my aunt and another woman who was hiding there with us, but they left my mother alone with us three small boys clinging to her.

I was too young to know why they had taken the women away. In time the women returned, crying, but their tears meant nothing to me since I had seen many tears, often from women who had lost their whole families in a matter of seconds.

The Moroccans forced my grandfather to bake for them. They supplied the ingredients and he was able to skim a little flour, margarine, or yeast off the top, even though he was told that he would be shot if caught. With the yeast, which was virtually unobtainable, my mother ventured out to the farming villages to trade for some eggs or milk. This *hamstern*, as it was called, was strictly forbidden but she had no choice since everyone was hungry, especially the children.

My brother Klaus stayed home most of the time, but Martin would join me on scrounging missions and sometimes we would bring home chocolate or a piece of soap. When the soldiers lined up in the schoolyard, some of my friends and I would squeeze our arms through the standing line of smelly, jabbering men and hold out our dented milk containers toward the man with the soup ladle. He was usually not watching very closely and filled our cans mechanically, just as he did for the soldiers.

Sometimes the Moroccans would bring in sheep from the fields and slaughter them in the creek bed. We hid behind the large rocks and watched the entire procedure. They first stuck a bayonet into the sheep's throat, and once it had bled to death, they blew it up from behind and beat it with sticks. They then cut the animal up, discarding the liver and heart, which they threw into the bushes. The fight was on then—kids emerged from everywhere, trying to get the discards. Many times I won and proudly raced home with my loot, but my mother invariably spanked me with a rubber hose for having been gone all day.

Gradually, conditions improved. The Marshall Plan went into effect and we children were fed a cup of watery chocolate with a piece of bread each day, and given a Hershey bar every Thursday morning at eleven o'clock. When winter came, however, there were no extra clothes. For two years I had been wearing the same pair of shorts that my mother had made from a flag and I had no shoes. We were always cold and hungry, but we survived. This experience as a child in Germany was my first lesson in survival.

From Calw to Vietnam via the United States Air Force may seem a strange route but it happened quite naturally. After seeing an advertisement in an American magazine showing two small airplanes with the legend "We need men to fly these planes," I made up my mind that I was going to fly one of them.

I importuned an American relative to sponsor me and to lend me some of the money I would need. The rest of the money I earned. Along with fifteen other apprentices, I worked for a tool and die maker and helped build gigantic clocks and faceplates for cathedrals all over Germany. Our boss was a hard and cruel taskmaster who would beat us with his calloused hands that were accustomed to forging metal on an anvil. Herman Hesse, who was born in Calw, ran away from this very shop years before I was compelled to do the same. But perhaps this harsh treatment prepared me for my prison guards in the Laotian jungle.

I finally made it to the United States and joined the air force where I was promised that I would be going to a flight training school in Texas. I did indeed have my first flight—to San Antonio—but it was also my last. After that we drilled unceasingly and the only airplanes I saw were the ones displayed at Lackland Air Force Base. Our entire battalion was assigned to the motor pool at various places.

Years later I took and passed the test offered to enlisted men who wanted to become pilots. I had become a United States citizen but my four years ran out before I was assigned to a flying class. By then I had a new goal: to pass the entrance test to the navy flight course at Pensacola. This I did, and after extensive training I received orders to Vietnam.

1 CRASH

Not long after leaving Alameda Naval Air Station, the last place I was stationed in California, I put together my personal survival gear from the kit issued to all pilots, adding those items that I thought might be of more help to me. I included lots of medicine, yellow tablets which were supposed to be good for just about everything, salt tablets, and pep pills. Beef jerky, pepperoni, and sugared nuts were also stashed away neatly in my new survival vest. This vest wrapped completely around my chest and hung by straps from my shoulders, and anything in it had to be arranged in such a way that the buckles from the parachute shoulder straps would lie flat and not press against the body during pullout or high-G maneuvers. I also wanted a mosquito net and rain poncho, but neither was on the carrier. I asked our parachute rigger to make a sack by sewing together two three-foot by six-foot dark green nylon sheets and running a zipper across the top. I cut a fist-sized hole on each side of this bag and glued a mosquito netting over it. This way I could zip myself in and breathe at night without bugs crawling over me. I taped the flat and neatly folded bag to the back of my survival vest. It eventually became my most prized possession.

I next pretended that I had lost my identification card and requested a new one. Although against regulations during flights, I wore my German climbing boots which I had taken apart in order to insert my original I.D. card inside the sole of one and a Geneva Convention card in the other. I also split the double tongue and hid a $100 bill in each shoe, thinking that the money might be good for a bribe. I glued everything back together and the boots looked just as they had before. I also had my old, invalid German passport with which I had emigrated to the United States, as well as my German birth certificate and other papers showing me to be a machinist. I wrapped these in plastic along with two pictures—one of my mother and the other of myself, sitting on my motorcycle with a European license plate.

As we were going north to Yankee Station, I adopted the name "Wilson" for my survival plans. I changed the name on my flight helmet, my flight suit, and all my other gear, from Dengler to Wilson. I also wore a short-sleeved shirt, a light pair of tan pants, and a very light summer jacket under my flight suit. In case I was shot down, some of the most important items would be in this light jacket—medicine, a knife, a signal mirror, a small cake of medicinal soap, fish hooks and line, flint and stone. In this way I might be able to pass as a German. The Vietnamese would search for Wilson after finding the aircraft, helmet, and flight suit, and not for me. I would try to pass as a civilian named "Dengler." If this were to fail, I would still have my I.D. card inside my boots to show that I was an American pilot and would therefore come under the Geneva Conventions.

On February 1, 1966, our skipper took the first flight in and returned with several panels shot out of his wing, and other pilots, also stationed on the carrier, were shot down. I was glad that I was duty officer and did not have to fly a sortie that first day.

The next day I was scheduled for the 0900 launch. There were four of us—the flight leader and myself, the section leader named "Spook," and his wingman. We spent a nearly sleepless night, and about three hours before the flight we had a thorough briefing. I went up to the flight deck and checked my aircraft to make sure everything was in order. The fuel tanks were full and the safety wires on the bombs were properly installed.

We finally manned our Skyraiders—the Douglas single-engine, propeller-driven bomber usually called the "Spad," but also christened with nicknames such as "Dauntless II," "BT2D-1," "AD," "A-1," or "Able Dog."

I switched my radio to Gray Eagle Approach. "This is Skyraider 04," I said. "Up and ready." By this time the jets had been launched and the four of us taxied forward. I revved up my engine on number three catapult, checked the gauges, put on full power, and saluted. With a jolt the catapult slung me off the carrier toward North Vietnam.

Heavily loaded with bombs and fuel, we flew northwest. In twenty minutes the coast of Vietnam came into sight. The weather over the ocean was fine, but over the coast it was all black. Coastal monsoons, the fierce rains I came to know so well, were blanketing the coast. Since the weather was so bad, we automatically tightened our formation to about three to four feet, wing to wing, but even flying that close I could not see Spook flying lead. We climbed through 700 feet in the soup and I was barely able to see the number two man. We knew there were mountains around us, so the leader was forced to turn back and lead us out toward the ocean, starting his climb immediately. We finally broke out of the clouds but the heavy weather made our primary target, a road with a truck convoy on it, impossible, so we headed for our alternate.

We crossed Vietnam above the clouds and penetrated halfway across Laos, flying over the Mugia Pass. The weather soon got better and we could make out the ground as we neared the alternate target. I had never seen anything like that green jungle, with an occasional row of sharp, white-looking cliffs rising up at least 2,000 feet. It looked exactly as I had read—impenetrable jungle. "If I ever get shot down over this, I will never make it out," I thought to myself.

I changed my altitude and heading every few seconds so that the radar-controlled guns on the ground would not be able to lock onto me. I was getting more and more separated from the rest of the flight as tailend Charlie, even though I had pushed the throttle all the way up. I glanced quickly at my map and at our location, trying to compare the ground to the map, but everything down there looked the same and I couldn't make out where I was. I stuffed the bulky, unfolded map down next to the seat, concentrating on staying with the others. We had flown nearly due west long enough to be over Laos, the flat ground that lay before me now. The air was dry and yellow, reminding me of the smog over Los Angeles. I found out later that it was due to the burning of the fields.

We were nearing our target. With the exception of the red master switch, all the arming switches for my bombs were set. Suddenly I heard Spook on my headset call out, "Zero seven, rolling in." I flicked on my master switch and tried to find the target myself, a road intersection with reported antiaircraft emplacements next to it. Up and to my left I saw Spook's bombs explode, a one-run load. An enormous dust cloud marked where the intersection must have been located. I was at 9,000 feet, much too close to the target to make my run. I had to yaw and steeply bank the aircraft three or four times since the intersection disappeared below the nose of the Spad, when it should have disappeared below the left wing root. When I thought I was in the right spot, I rolled in to the left to a nearly inverted position. Just then my AD lurched and began to shake violently. I let go of the throttle, knowing that I was hit, and grabbed the stick with both hands, yelling at the top of my lungs. I tried to radio to the rest of the flight but everything was dead--no sidetone, no click, nothing. The nose of my plane had fallen through, pointing nearly straight down. The antiaircraft emplacement came directly into view below me since the dust clouds had drifted away. I took an erratic aim and let go of my load by pulling the emergency release handle. The plane jumped up with the weight of the bombs gone as I pulled hard on the stick to bring the nose up toward the horizon. Two more blinding explosions off my right wingtip threw the aircraft totally out of control. My hands darted all over the cockpit, not knowing where they were going, while I was trying to remember emergency procedures. My engine was dead and I decided to jump.

The AD was not designed with an ejection seat. The canopy had to be blown open with the emergency air bottle. As the aircraft gyrated through the sky, I unstrapped myself, threw the harness out into the windstream, and lowered the seat. I started to climb onto the seat, staying crouched so the slipstream would not get hold of me. The unguided plane went through its own motions now, knocking me back and forth in the cockpit. Another nearby explosion made the plane shiver from nose to tail, and it was then that I decided to ride her in, no matter what. Haphazardly I strapped myself back in after I had unbuckled all the chute straps, so as not to get entangled or trapped after the crash.

There was a long green mountain ridge to my right. I thought that if I could get over it and into the next valley, as far away as possible from whoever was at the road junction, I would have a chance of escaping. It was risky since I was already low and did not know whether there would be an open clearing on the other side where I could ditch. I wobbled toward the ridge, losing too much altitude, and by now it looked as though I was going to crash into it. Because of the windmilling propeller I could still drop the flaps, allowing the aircraft to balloon over the ridge with only a few feet to spare. I threw out my authenticator, notes, and all my maps over this jungle ridge, while my eyes searched frantically for a place to belly in. There were a few huts down to my left and a tiny clearing about half a mile in front of me. Except for the clearing, it was an unending jungle of trees and was not the valley I had expected. Jumping was out of the question because I was too low.

Amazingly, I could still control the plane. I swung right, then a little to the left, then right again, trying to lose altitude, skidding in a half circle, aiming for the small clearing. The stick had to be kept almost all the way to the right to keep my wings somewhat level. By now I was at about 500 feet and a quarter mile from the clearing—close enough to see that I had made the wrong decision. The clearing was nothing more than a section of cut forest, studded with five-foot-high tree stumps. Later I learned that the villagers built their huts on top of the tree stumps to avoid the floodwaters and also to provide shelter below for their animals.

My mind and hands went confusedly through the crash procedures. My airspeed indicator erratically showed 160 knots—at least 60 knots too fast—but there was no way of slowing the monster down. I had to get the plane into the clearing. The wall of jungle trees at the end of the clearing grew larger and larger as I approached it rapidly. With both hands, I pushed the stick into the right forward corner of the cockpit to lose altitude. A completely bare tree, 150 feet tall with only three or four limbs, loomed directly in my path. I could not fly over it without crashing into the dense jungle beyond, so I boresighted the lower part of the dead tree. Just then I noticed the white tips of my external fuel tanks sticking out from under the wings. I yanked the emergency tank handle and dropped them off. It was a lucky thing that I had seen them because each carried 100 gallons of gas. The instant the weight was gone, the plane lifted upward, exactly the opposite of what I wanted. The stumps were just below the aircraft now and the tree was dead ahead. Hitting the tree straight on would snap it off and crush me inside the cockpit, so just before I hit I kicked the left rudder with all my strength, yawing the plane to take the full impact on my right wing root.

Tree and plane met with a violent shudder, tearing both apart. The left wing had swung forward and down, its tip snagging the ground, slamming the nose of the plane into the earth. The stick was torn out of my hands as all eight tons of Spad bounced back into the air, then tumbled over and over in a cartwheeling fashion. A stump ripped out the right side of the cockpit where the radios were, barely missing my leg. The force of deceleration pulled my helmet halfway across my face, then ripped it off. The inch-thick windscreen broke from its left corner in slow motion, like safety glass, and I ducked as the flying glass narrowly missed my head. I began to scream when I smelled oil and gas. Then, in a blur, I saw the entire tail section tumble by. I kept on yelling with my eyes closed, pressing my arms in front of my face, through the endless grinding and tearing. Then everything was silent.

What remained of the plane was lying almost completely rolled over. I was wedged between the jammed bars of the canopy rail of the twisted cockpit. Confused and in a daze, I was hanging nearly upside down by my straps. The cockpit was filled with heavy green foliage and thick dust cut off most of the light. The dust filled my mouth and lungs and started me coughing. Seconds after the crash I still expected a fire and an explosion. Frantically, I tugged and pulled to get out, but I could barely move. After that, I don't know what happened.

As if reemerging into life I came to, lying on my back about a hundred feet from the crash. My Mae West was gone—I must have torn it off. Stumbling and falling like a drunkard, I crawled away as fast as I could, occasionally glancing back, expecting the fire that never came. When I reached the edge of the clearing and started into the bush, I stood up and took a quick look at what could still be seen of the fallen and broken bird. A thin veil of dust hung limply around her. There was not a sound.

2 CAPTURE

My plane was down behind enemy lines in Laos. Someone must have seen or heard me, since on the way down I had spotted huts not more than a quarter mile from the crash. It was important to put distance between myself and the aircraft. The enemy would probably expect me to go west, toward Thailand, right away. I decided to go north for a day or so and then head west.

The country was flat and the woods were open with an occasional patch of thick jungle around which one could work his way fairly easily. I soon was out of breath and my throat was dry, but I kept running toward a heavily wooded area and did not dare stop. Once inside, I came to a foul-smelling creek, with stagnant rust-colored pools. The sandy banks went down about twenty feet to the water. The dust was as fine as powder, and I sank up to my knees in it. I really needed a drink but kept thinking about the dysentery and other diseases that might result from drinking the water. I decided against quenching my thirst.

After crossing the shallow stream it was difficult to climb the opposite bank. The dust was deep as quicksand and I kept sliding back down, stuck sometimes up to my waist. I crawled downstream on my belly through the pools for a few hundred feet and finally managed to get out by clambering up the trunk of a fallen tree. In the heat the mud caked on me instantly. Then I realized that my knee was hurt and the mud that I pulled away from my neck was bloody. Feeling around, I found a small piece of glass from the canopy stuck behind my right ear. I sat down on a fallen log and pulled up my trousers. My knee was deep purple and very painful to the touch. I would do something about it later.

Now I had to get my wits together and stick to some plan to evade pursuit. The thick green foliage all around was great camouflage for the time being. I took off my green navy flight suit and survival vest, which left me in my light trousers, short-sleeved shirt, and tan jacket. They had already dried and felt stiff as a board. I transferred all the things I thought I might need from my survival vest to my jacket, then got rid of the mud in my shoes and laced them up tightly, feeling for the money hidden inside. The silence was broken by a tearing metal sound in the direction of my airplane. I jumped behind the log, checked my .38 revolver and laid it beside the survival radio, not daring to move for a few minutes—but there were no more sounds. I needed some sort of bandage for my injured knee. Quickly I picked up some sticks, held them to the right and left of my leg, and wrapped an elastic bandage from my gear around it.

While buttoning my jacket, I was jolted by the sound of a rifle blast, and bullets hit all around me. Another burst smashed into the trees behind me as I dove into the underbrush. "Automatic weapons" flashed through my mind. I had turned and noticed the radio and the .38 on the log. We had been told that if a helicopter pilot hears a beep from such a survival radio, he comes in without hesitation. Should my pursuers obtain the radio, they certainly would use it to bag a helicopter. In fact, Duane Martin, later a prison camp companion of mine, was shot down that way, homing in on a distress signal. The radio had to be destroyed.

The way the enemy was shooting and hollering, I knew they had seen and surrounded me. I crawled back along the log, grabbed the radio and slammed the blade of my heavy survival knife completely through it. I then shoved it, with the revolver and the rest of my gear, underneath the log next to me, covering it all up with a few handfuls of dirt and leaves. Tense with fear, I carefully crawled away, dragging my green sleeping bag behind me. People yelled to each other in the bush to my right, so I kept crawling to the left. There was a sound very close by and something moved. I pressed my head to the ground and stayed absolutely still. Leathery, dark brown feet walked by a yard away. My first Pathet Lao was far different from anything I had anticipated. He was small and had muscular, calloused feet and his right leg was shorter than his left. He wore only a loincloth and in his hand he carried a long-bladed machete. Slowly I pulled the sleeping bag over my body for camouflage and cursed my stupidity in leaving the .38 behind. I thought of going back for my gear, but feared the thought of capture. The sound of the shouting moved farther and farther away and I began to crawl in the opposite direction of their shouts. I swung around to get my survival gear, but then decided against it, especially since I had damaged the radio. "Hell, I have my pepperoni, medicine, shoes, and other important things with me in my jacket," I mumbled to myself. I turned and crawled away for about half a mile.

As I began to think about the fix I was in, I nearly panicked and had to force myself to think constructively. Escape and survival were not unknown to me. Since boyhood in Germany the war and its aftermath had taught me to fend for myself. As a boy scout I had gone on long marches and trips, living off the land. In the navy, I went through survival school at Warner Springs, California, and was the first to escape successfully three times. Thinking of my past reassured me. I told myself, "I'll walk right out of here in nothing flat." I ignored the pain in my leg and went on.

I took my bearings from the sun and using a small navy compass that I had attached to my watchband, I started north, traveling slowly in a crouched position, stopping every five or six steps to listen. Somewhere to my right a girl was singing. I looked around but saw only a section of an old bamboo fence.

It was hot. I had been in San Antonio, Texas, in the middle of summer, but that didn't seem nearly as hot as this. "It must be at least 120 degrees," I thought, and now the heat, dehydration, and mosquitoes were driving me nearly mad.

The animal trail I had been following curved to the right, back in the direction of the girl's voice. I backtracked and took a different trail that led in the opposite direction.

I stayed on the trail until it led to a clearing in the jungle that was all blackened, as if it had been burned. A tall fence built out of logs and covered with blackberry bushes stood to the left of the clearing. Walking beside that fence I came to a large bamboo cove where another fence came in at an angle to form a giant funnel. There were village sounds of dogs, chickens, and children coming from its other side. I steadied myself on some bamboo and peeked around a thick cluster into the cove. Suddenly the make-believe ground I was standing on gave way and I was left swinging from the bamboo, only a few feet above a bed of sticks with razor-sharp points, stuck in the ground at one-foot intervals. Rapidly I swung myself free of the animal trap.

I finally made it through the clearing by crawling on my stomach. Someone had left a small gate open to my left, leading from the clearing toward the heavier brush close by. The next thing I knew, I was crawling under a partly collapsed hut with one corner still about four feet off the ground. I stopped and listened, but all was quiet. Slowly I stood up to have a look inside and it was all I could do to keep from vomiting. In the hut was a human corpse, probably dead for weeks. Its lower body was gone, as was most of the face, and the big, round eye sockets were empty. It was covered by thousands of ants and maggots. The thought of leprosy streaked through my mind and I decided to get out of there, fast. I fumbled in my jacket to be sure my medicinal soap was still there so I could wash myself at the next creek. I found out later what ants can do and how quickly, and then realized that the man probably had not been dead for more than two days.

No matter which way I went I could not get away from signs of village life. Only a few hours had passed since I had nearly been shot and I had already forgotten about it. I came to a small, muddy creek, but since a villager was nearby, I thought it unsafe to cross there and silently walked along the creek for about half a mile until it spilled into a wide river. Standing on a large sandbar were at least fifteen water buffalo with great curved horns. They were the first I had ever seen and I was not sure whether they would attack if I got too close.

A little farther on I came to another impenetrable log fence with thorny brush growing all over it. Slowly, so as not to fall into another animal trap, I backtracked and eased myself into the river under the buffalos' watchful eyes. I was hardly into the water when I decided it would be better to cross after night had fallen. I spotted a small hiding place in a hollow high up on the river bank which looked as though it had been dug out by water, but that was hardly possible since it was at least twenty feet above water level. Little did I know then how monsoon rains could turn a small creek into a raging river in a matter of hours.

Once in the hollow I sat on my bag, took off my shoes and socks, shook out the dirt that had gotten into everything, and ate some pepperoni. Thirst had been with me constantly and the pepperoni made it even worse, but I didn't want to take the chance of being seen while getting a drink from the stream. I must have sat there for about thirty minutes before I again changed my mind about fording the river and decided to take my chances. I stripped naked and stuffed all my clothes into my green bag, quickly slid down the bank, and hurried across the sand into the water. The buffalo did nothing more than look at me, then slowly turned and walked away, their ugly, whitish bellies gently swaying with the rhythm of their walk.

The water felt great, cool and refreshing after all that heat. The current was getting stronger as I waded deeper and deeper until the water was up to my neck. I made it across and tried to climb out but the bank was too muddy and gooey. Whenever I thought I had reached solid ground, the mud would crumble and suck me down, back into the river. I finally threw my bag out first, and with all my strength slid myself out of the hip-deep mud onto the bank.

I scooped some water into my shoe and dropped an iodine tablet into it. The tablet dissolved slowly and the spot where it lay was clearly outlined by a dark, yellow circle. I hurried up the process with a stick and drank the yellow water down greedily. Without a doubt, that yellow, bitter water was the best I had ever had and immediately gave me renewed strength.

Everything was so silent, so peaceful. Sometimes I looked up, hoping to see an aircraft, but none appeared. It was getting late in the afternoon and I began thinking about a place to spend the night. In one of the clearings I came upon a small waterhole in which a water buffalo was covered up to its head in the muddy water. Nearby I found a good spot that overlooked the clearing; in case an aircraft flew over, I could easily run out and wave to it. As soon as I stopped moving the mosquitoes attacked without mercy. I crawled into my sleeping bag for protection, but since there was not enough air inside and the sweat ran down my body in rivers, I lasted there only a few minutes. The heat and mosquitoes forced me to decide against staying there for the night, so I put on my shoes and moved on.

Soon, the sound of chickens cackling and a dog barking in the distance warned me that I was approaching another village. I was not worried about being seen because it was getting dark, and the tall elephant grass through which I was pushing was great protection. The first star had appeared in the evening sky when, as I stood in the middle of the field, the familiar sound of AD engines filled the air. I frantically tried to get out of the grass to signal them, but when I reached the clearing the aircraft were gone. They had passed directly overhead, no higher than two hundred feet, weaving back and forth. I didn't take it too hard, as I knew they were searching for me and would be back. If only I had had a flare with me I would have been back on the carrier in time for dinner, but the flares were back under the log with the rest of the gear I had hidden.

Exhausted from the day and suddenly in complete despair, I swept a patch of ground covered with sticks and pebbles, slipped into my bag, and fell asleep within minutes.

I was suddenly wide awake, my body frozen with fear, my heart beating loudly. Something heavy was crawling up my legs as I lay there, zipped in my bag, motionless. Visions of all kinds of animals and snakes flashed through my mind. I kicked hard with both legs and screamed as loudly as I could. The animal, whatever it was, jumped off me and crashed through the bush as I sat up. It was impossible for me to go back to sleep and that first, cold night in the jungle seemed endless.

Daybreak finally came and without hesitation I moved on.

I crossed two very narrow trails before I realized what they were. I followed the second one for at least a quarter of a mile, thinking that no one would be on a trail at that time of morning, but then left it because it went straight north. I licked the dew clinging to the plants and leaves and sucked on my wet clothes. Three huge birds that looked like vultures sat on the trail head and if I had had my gun, I would have been eating shortly. A gun, however, would have made too much of a racket and would have given my position away, so perhaps it was best that I didn't have the temptation.

I came to a small clearing with what looked like a few deserted huts built on stilts. I debated whether to take the risk and venture into one of the huts to look for food. Hunger won over caution. Carrying my shoes so as not to leave any boot prints in the fine, half-inch dust around the huts, I crawled up to the back of the hut nearest the edge of the clearing and slipped underneath it to the front porch. As with most of these huts, the porch was built about five feet off the ground. I grabbed a makeshift ladder that was lying beneath the hut and climbed up onto the porch. Hurriedly I untied the rattan that held the flimsy, doorlike entry together and stepped inside, pulling the shutter closed behind me. Whoever had built the hut had left about a six-inch space between the roof and the frame for ventilation and this opening made a great vantage point from which to see if anyone had seen me enter. I saw nothing except five other huts, two frames of burned-out huts and what looked like a river gully in the distance. The inside of the small hut had been blackened by smoke from the open fireplace in the corner. I stuck my hand into it but it was cold. A few shelves built along one wall were held up by rattan and filled with old woven baskets thrown there at random. In one corner hung a huge basket filled with beautiful blue orchids that cascaded down like a miniature waterfall. Three bottles, similar to the beer bottles I knew in Germany, hung on the wall. Two of them had been plugged with small corncobs and I took down the cleanest one, dark green in color, and put it by the door. On the other side, lying on the floor, were what looked like potatoes, so I filled my pockets. I grabbed the bottle, glanced outside to make sure no one was around, and pushed out through the flap, which fell back into place just as it had been when I got there. I returned the ladder to where I had found it under the hut, and with a piece of brush I swished out my tracks. Happy now with some food and a water container, I put on my shoes and headed west.

After traveling through a thick, tick-infested area, I came to the river I had seen from the hut, which was probably the same one I had crossed the day before. I slid down its thirty-foot embankment, filled the bottle with sand and water, and shook it wildly to scour and wash it. It was soon clean enough to fill with water and I dropped in a few iodine tablets. I then quickly washed myself with the medicinal soap. Alarming sounds came from the brush next to me, making me freeze, and a large pig came dashing out of the undergrowth, followed by four smaller ones. They did not resemble domestic pigs, but had long snouts and short black bodies like the havelinas of Texas and Mexico. I squatted quietly at the edge of the water and hoped the sow would not pick up my scent, as I was not certain whether or not she would attack. However, she only looked at me, grunted, and proceeded on her way.

My bath had made me feel better but the night's chill still hanging in the air quelled any desire to get into the water and cross the river. Slipping and sliding up the bank, I came across another small trail. Following it a few hundred yards, I heard voices not far away. There in front of me was the straw roof of a large hut, sticking out above the thick elephant grass and bamboo that formed a solid, impenetrable wall on either side of the trail. I turned around and dashed down the path, passing the small gully where I had come from the river. I recognized the drone of an aircraft in the distance as the sound of a Spad. I ran back to the gully, the only place where the jungle canopy opened in the direction of the familiar engine sound. Just as I got there the plane flew directly overhead, barely missing the treetops. A second one approached, and I began waving my arms like a madman as he zoomed directly over me at a few hundred feet. My heart sank. The thought that I should have stayed near my aircraft instead of wandering off flashed through my mind. My eyes kept looking after the planes, afraid they were flying away, but soon the first Spad banked and headed my way.

I was wild with joy! Running back toward one of the burned-out huts, I tore off my shirt to get to my white T-shirt, broke off a piece of a half-burned bamboo ladder, stuck my T-shirt on it, and waved the flag frantically. The second aircraft turned and began to follow the first one toward me, but they then made a climbing left turn to a higher altitude, too high to see me. I was sick. On the first pass they had been so close that our VA-145 squadron insignia slashed on the sides, the sword with a lion, could easily be seen.

Still waving my shirt, I saw in the distance two more Spads and two Jolly Green Giant helicopters joining the original two airplanes about three miles to the east. It was a search party, all right, looking for me. If only I had had my signaling mirror, which had also been hidden under the log, I could have easily signaled them, as the sun was now directly in my face. Again a Spad turned and headed directly toward me. I was exhilarated! "I'm spotted, I'm spotted!" My heart pumped wildly. Directly overhead now, he rocked his wings back and forth, while I swung my flag in a great circle, sure that he had seen me. A C-54, a four-engine command bird, then approached from way up west. I wondered then if the Spad was only waving hello to the C-54.

I ran back to a hut, heedless of danger, and climbed up on the frame, thinking that this jungle was too thick a camouflage for them to see me. At that one moment, which lasted forever, I knew I had been spotted. Spotted, indeed, but by the Pathet Lao. I jumped off the frame and ran for my life to the river and down the embankment, dove headlong into the water and swam hard and fast to the other side. With each stroke I kept thinking, "Get to the other side before they reach the bank."

It had been a mutual discovery. When they saw me, I saw them. From all the yelling and commotion in the tall grass, I guessed there must be many of them. Reaching the other side of the stream, I had no trouble this time climbing the muddy wall of the bank with my bad leg, even though it was steeper than the other side. I pressed myself close to the ground and looked back across the river to see the guerrillas emerge from the grass, following my tracks, which were all too clear in the soft earth. One of them pointed in my direction and after some discussion, they disappeared back into the tall grass. Looking downstream, I spotted a raft and thought they might be going for it to cross the river. I turned and ran through an open area and then down between neatly planted rows of banana trees. I moved on at a steady pace, but no one seemed to be following me.

Everything was quiet, except for the intermittent whirring of cicadas. In my hurry I stumbled across a hut in the middle of nowhere but luckily no one was around. To catch my breath, I sat down underneath the hut and pulled some leaches off my legs. A large basketful of chickens caught my eye and I didn't waste any time grabbing the largest of the lot and, without killing it, dropped it into my bag and continued on my way. A little farther on was another hut, but so well camouflaged that I literally bumped into it. As I hurried by the hut I grabbed a handful of ash from the fireplace to check for the telltale warmth of a recent fire. Instantly some of the skin of my hand was burned off by the red embers I had picked up and which were hidden under the grey ash of the fire. Somebody had been there very recently. I hurried away and hid myself for a moment at the edge of the small area that was cleared in front of the hut. At that moment a small woman dressed in black came around the corner toward the hut and stopped alongside it. She looked back, calling someone, and a small child came around the corner. She lovingly placed her arms around the child and they walked off. She didn't act as if she had seen me but that was too close. I vowed again to be more careful. The first thing I did was to let the chicken go since I didn't want to be caught with stolen goods.

It was difficult to avoid trails, as they seemed to be everywhere. Very slowly and carefully I worked my way through the brush trying not to make any noise at all, finally arriving at an open intersection of several trails. Looking quickly to the left and right to make sure the way was clear, I ran across the trails in a crouched position, toward the heavy brush twenty feet away. Halfway across I heard someone yelling, *"Yute, Yute!"* and just by the sound of it, I knew it was meant for me. I turned my head and met the cold steel gaze of an M-1 rifle, pointed directly at my face.

3 MARCH

My hands shot up in the air and I didn't dare move because I knew I would be nailed on the spot. *"Nicht schiessen, nicht schiessen,"* I yelled, hoping to pass for a German civilian. Another man ran up to the Laotian with the M-1 and they yelled something into the air and the bush came alive with people. "That's the end of me," I thought, waiting for a bullet to hit. Two of them gestured to me to move in their direction. Very cautiously, so as not to stumble and spook them into shooting me, I obliged.

Someone hit me on the back of the head with a rifle butt, knocking me to the ground, then pressed the muzzle of the gun against my neck. I shut my eyes, while one of them began searching me. The man that held the rifle to my neck while his friend searched me was dressed comically in black sunglasses, U.S. Army sweater, a U.S. green fatigue jacket, rolled-up brown pants, and light blue rubber boots that a woman would wear in the rain. I wondered what in the hell was going on, with them wearing U.S. clothes. For a moment I thought they might be friendly troops mistaking me in my civilian clothes for the enemy.

The man holding the rifle at me had produced an American .38 revolver, waving it in my face. The second man was dressed more like one of the villagers, several of whom had arrived at the scene. They stood there, not saying a word, just watching. My wrist was tied with a simple slipknot, jerked up across my back, and the rope wound around my neck down to my other arm. The oddly dressed man gave the rope a vicious jerk and pointed in the direction we were to go. We went a few hundred yards to a clearing where they motioned me to sit down, untied me and again searched me. One man pulled out the potatoes I had stolen from the hut and, pointing to them, he hit his forehead with the palm of his hand, saying, *"Ba, ba!"* many times, as he threw them away. I waited to be clobbered for stealing but they did nothing. Three weeks later I learned that they were not potatoes, after all, but opium balls, which would probably have killed me if I had eaten them.

I then showed them my German passport, continuously speaking to them in German. The one in the blue boots took away all of my papers and stuffed them into his rucksack, which had appeared from nowhere. Someone seized the bottle with the iodine tablets. They did not recognize the razor blades in the dispenser and let me keep them, along with the razor and the pepperoni. They were constantly looking around, impatient for me to hurry and get all my stuff out.

To my surprise, they did not take away my water bottle or my shoes; I had expected to lose everything. The man with the .38 pistol then pointed to my watch, which I did not mind losing, but I wanted to keep the compass underneath it by pulling it off the cotton band. He took both, then pointed to the ring that Marina, my fiancée, had given me. I shook my head, so he started to kick me and demand it over and over again, but I refused. Two of them got in a squabble over the ring and they settled the argument by letting me keep it.

I was jerked to my feet and retied. A man in a loincloth joined us and we began running. The pain, particularly in my left leg, was intense but I was not allowed to slow down. My legs started cramping and I collapsed, sick to my stomach from the murderous heat, the lack of food, and all the running. One of the guerillas stood over me and put his M-1 rifle to my forehead, yelling, *"Bie, bie!"* I made it for another mile before collapsing again. Once more he put his muzzle to my head, but with the cramps and my arms tied behind me, I just couldn't move. One of the men began massaging my legs and after five minutes they both jerked me up by the rope, kicked me in the back, and on we went.

We ran from late morning until well into the evening. How I made it, I'll never know. We changed guides twice and by the time we had arrived at our destination, there were nine armed guards, a village guide, and myself. Other men had gathered in a clearing, none of whom looked like soldiers since each was dressed differently. The man in charge—the honcho—dressed in a brown uniform and wearing a belt buckle emblazoned with a red star, came up close and eyed me. His gaze made me shift uneasily. Suddenly he pointed a finger at me and shouted, "Bang, bang!" I drew back in surprise and he smiled with pleasure at his little joke. He then pointed to my wrist and I nodded to the oddly dressed fellow who had taken my watch. Searching for a few minutes in his rucksack, he came up with my watch, passport, and all my other papers and handed them to the leader. While he was inspecting my things I spoke to him in German, but he didn't understand English, much less German. He took a pepperoni, smelled it, and indicated for me to take a bite and then he had a taste. He immediately spit it out and slapped me on the head.

Three guards took me over to a tree, tied my hands together behind it, and then tied my ankles. Satisfied with their work, they sat down in front of me and cocked their rifles a few times to show me that they meant business. I watched the leader put my passport and papers in his small cap, which reminded me of those I had seen Chinese soldiers wearing in movies.

I was left alone except for two guards sitting next to me, smoking their little bamboo pipes. For two days now I had had no food except the pepperoni and a few old sugared nuts I had discovered stuck to the inside of my pocket. Night fell but no dinner came to appease my intense hunger.

The guards finally untied me. One pulled a pepperoni from my jacket and stuck it into my mouth. They then drove four stakes into the ground and tied me spread-eagled to them. Even before they were half finished, the rocks and sticks poking my back made me terribly uncomfortable. I was then left alone with the moon. Tears came into my eyes as I thought of home but soon sleep came over me. I slept deeply, to be awakened only occasionally by the mosquitoes, the ants, and the infrequent sound of an aircraft which made me sad and the guards jumpy.

The sun had already climbed over the horizon by the time I awoke. My face was such a swollen mass of mosquito bites that I could hardly see and my entire body was covered with ants. I had read about Indians doing these things to frontiersmen, staking them out to be tortured by insects, but I never imagined that it would happen to me. I let my guards know that I was awake because I had to relieve myself, but no one came. Everyone was sitting around the fire. "Hey you bastards," I yelled, "how about it?" I didn't care anymore whether I spoke German or English—I was in pain!

Half an hour later someone came but I had already gone in my pants. It made me furious but there was nothing I could do except give him a dirty look as he untied me. I sat up and stretched and found that both my arms were asleep. The guard held his nose and motioned me over toward the heavier underbrush. Two more guards joined us, carrying their weapons over their shoulders. I tried to clean my pants out as best I could but felt uncomfortable to be watched in the process. *"Bie!"* one shouted, so we left.

One of my original guards, the good-looking one who had seemed the most intelligent of the lot, had already departed. I credited him for my first meal—a handful of rice that one of them threw on the ground in front of me along with my filled bottle of water. I ate every kernel of rice while the guards sat around me without saying a word—just watched me eat like an animal with my arms tied behind me. I vowed to myself to get even with them—to kill them when I got the chance. The rest of the group, all heavily loaded with what appeared to be German hand grenades, ammunition, and blankets, gathered around my guards. Two live chickens, tied together by their legs, hung head down from a pole that supported a large basket of rice on either end. One of the guerillas brought my shoes, which had been taken away the evening before, and I felt pretty good that the money and I.D. card had not been discovered.

We started traveling through the woods, led by a villager who stayed with us until we got beyond his territory, and then was replaced by another from the next village. This continued for three weeks until we reached the prison camp. I was glad my leg wasn't broken, since I couldn't imagine how I would have kept up with them. The Pathet Lao were amazing, especially the women who, whenever they traveled with us, carried most of the loads. Their packs weighed at least fifty pounds but they never complained or sat down to rest. I saw only one woman wearing shoes—the rest went barefoot. All of them had stocky legs built up by carrying backbreaking loads from the time they could walk.

It was easy to travel across the flat terrain. Walking on the trails was not bad at all, as long as we were inside the jungle canopy, but in the open the heat was unbearable. I began drinking water madly. By midmorning on the second day I had polished off three bottles. Fortunately, the guards had returned my iodine tablets and I was able to purify the water. We crossed an area where missiles (probably from the LAU-32 missile container we had passed along the trail a while back) had recently pockmarked the earth. We were heading directly east, away from the area where I had crashed.

When the sun was straight overhead, we came across a narrow creek in a steep ravine and the group prepared to rest. The men took off their rucksacks and half of them undressed and ran to the creek, holding their privates in their hands to avoid exposure. After I lost the argument to wash out the foul smell of my pants, I sat down on the trail with my back against the wall that formed one side of the canyon. It was nice and cool there. My small share of rice was given to me on a banana leaf. When I got seconds, I became bold and asked for thirds, which they also gave me. It was sticky rice that caked into round balls. After a couple of months I got used to the half-cooked rice but it took hours to digest, especially if you had nothing else with it. Wherever we went, every villager carried a small basket of rice on his belt, usually right next to the long slim tube that held his machete. While I was eating, only one guard with his rifle across his lap kept an eye on me, but he sat too far away for me to try anything like jumping him.

The men returned from their bath. Once they had rewrapped their loincloths, we continued on. The jungle became so thick and the trail so overgrown that it had to be widened with machetes. We moved slowly so as not to fall into the small trenches and holes. It did not register until I saw empty mortar shells and hand grenade containers lying around that these holes led to tunnels, hiding places for the guerrillas. But where were the troops? On closer scrutiny, I realized that this station had been abandoned because the trails were so overgrown. I pulled out the leaves that were corking my water bottle and was about to take a drink when the skinny guard came over. Shaking his head, he pointed in the direction we were heading and described an arc from the sun to the horizon. "*Vomi, vomi,*" he cautioned me, pointing to the bottle. He was telling me that there would be no more waterholes until that evening.

"Where are they taking me?" Ever since my capture I had been trying to convince them that I was a friend so they might drop their guard and give me a chance to escape; but it was no use. "*Savanakhet?*" I said, pointing to myself and to the others. The guards pointed east in the direction of our travel. "*Savanakhet, Savanakhet,*" they said, nodding their heads. I knew that the town of Savanakhet was to the west and that they were lying. We were traveling east and I wondered whether they were taking me to North Vietnam. On the carrier we had heard some rumors about war criminal trials for pilots and about captured pilots dragged through the streets on public display. I quickly squelched that thought—I had enough to worry about already.

From the top of our ridge where the trees had been chopped down we had a magnificent view of the country that lay below. A large river wound its way like a snake through the country which was checkered into rice paddies, resembling the neatly kept farms back in Germany. I was suddenly very homesick.

I realized the river was the key to my escape. If I could get away this night and make it to the river, I would be able to float my way to freedom. We continued down the very steep trail into the valley.

With their heavy loads, the women had a difficult time keeping their balance. Though I did not have a load, my arms tied tightly behind my back did not afford me any balance either, and I fell most of the way down. When I had first seen these women I was startled by their blood-red lips and stained teeth. They were always spitting out what looked like blood and only after one of the women offered me some betel nuts did I realize that that was what caused the red stains. Just about every woman I saw chewed those nuts constantly.

The leaves plugging my water bottle had dried and fallen out, so on the way down, as we stopped to rest and I was untied, I grabbed some leaves to make a new bottle-stopper. The skinny guard came over and, shaking his head, indicated that I shouldn't use these leaves. He pointed to a bush whose leaves were safe to use. Any time I made a mistake like that, this guard was quick to correct me, which seemed to indicate they wanted me alive.

The sun was already low in the sky but we were only halfway down the mountain. My mouth felt puffy and dry from dust and thirst but my bottle was empty. My mind was on the river when somebody nudged me and, turning around, I saw a villager smiling at me and showing me a large compass. As he opened it up, I saw a mirror attached to the top cover. He gestured for me to have it and since the guards were so busy climbing down the trail, I felt safe in taking it from him. As luck would have it, however, one of the guards turned just in time to see the villager trying to pass it to me. He ran up, yelling threats, and clobbered the villager on the head. The villager then turned to the guard and apparently told him he was just trying to harass me by showing it to me. Evidently that satisfied the guards who had gathered around. They moved the villager up front and we continued down the hill. As the villager passed me to go forward, we exchanged glances and I was deeply touched by his sad expression—I knew he wanted to help. Later on I found out that quite a few of the villagers had been imprisoned by the Pathet Lao, accused of helping our side.

It was 7:35 P.M. on the leader's watch when we arrived at the bottom of the valley. The river looked much narrower than it had seemed from the top and the water was only about a foot deep and barely flowing. My hope began to fade—I certainly could not float down this ridiculous creek. As I looked downstream, however, I saw the stream join a much wider one, the one we had seen from the ridge. I filled my bottle, dropped a couple of tablets into the water, but could not wait and drank it down before the tablets had dissolved, leaving a terrible taste. We all sat down—the villagers in one group, the guards in another, and I, alone in the middle.

One of the guards left and returned a few minutes later accompanied by a tall fellow. I nodded my head and the tall man returned the greeting. After asking the guard some questions he turned to me and pointed to my pockets, which I carefully emptied, laying out the contents item by item on the ground. He studied each article and then picked up the razor blade dispenser. After fussing with it for a while he was finally able to wriggle a blade out. He rushed over to the skinny guard and proceeded to raise hell with him for not having taken away the blades from me. Since I was tied down constantly, the blades were of no advantage anyway, but I regretted losing them.

One of the men presented my passport to the tall man. Now he was really confused, since it didn't resemble anything he had seen before. He would not have known what he was looking at, even if it had been an American passport. He kept asking me for further identification, getting angrier and angrier the more I shook my head. At first I thought that I could pull off my fake identity with the Laotians, but there was no way since most of them could not write or read. I soon realized that it would be better if I showed him my navy I.D. card. I sat down and took off my shoes, pointing to the razor blades the honcho was holding in his hand, and made a cutting motion. He nodded and gave me one, which I used to cut part of the sole. The cards did not surprise him. In fact, his expression never changed and I gathered that he had seen this sort of card before. He gave the guards an order and they promptly came over to me, clicking the bolts on their rifles. They pointed the weapons at me and gave me dirty looks, waving their clenched fists in my face, and some even spitting at me. I knew that this was to be my execution. The leader took away all my pills and threw the pepperoni into the bush. Without warning, the guards pounced on me and began beating me with their rifle butts and fists, and then stopped as suddenly as they had started. Although the beating left me in terrible pain, I was not cut up too badly.

They staked me to the ground as they had done the first night. At least fifteen guards stayed around me and smoked their pipes all night long, the bowl's yellow glow lighting up each man's face as he took a drag. The stars were beautiful, and I wondered if Marina was looking up then, too.

Early in the morning I was untied and given rice, and my wallet, pictures, and the iodine tablets. Much to my surprise, the thirteen dollars I had in my wallet was untouched. I was then assigned two permanent guards. They wore purple-blue uniforms, high-top tennis shoes, and a piece of white parachute cloth wrapped around their necks. "Tan" was the Laotian name of the taller one and the other I nicknamed "Bastard." From now on the party never numbered less than five in all and that morning there were nineteen. We left early, before the sun had risen, mainly to take advantage of the morning cool.

By now I had begun to yearn for the sound of my own language. Most of all I needed to find out what was going to happen to me. Where was I being taken? I wished I could speak at least a few words of Laotian so I could tell them when I had to go to the bathroom. I had a bad case of dysentery which had become an annoying problem both for me and for them.

After a few minutes' walk from the camp we arrived at the river and all of us washed. The river bed was at least 200 feet wide but the dry season had reduced the river to a mere trickle of water flowing sluggishly between the rocks. We walked in the river bed—nineteen men strung out like a caravan going through the desert—eight in front of me, ten in back. I had a hard time keeping my balance with my hands tied behind me and occasionally slipped on the moss-covered rocks and fell into the muddy pools of water that had gathered in low spots. The guards would laugh loudly to each other and point to me.

Soon the morning cool was gone and the sun was beating down. We were now traveling in the open without any shade since the village guide had led us out of the river bed and into the rice paddies. The mud in the rice paddies was as dry and hard as cement and nothing was growing in them. We walked atop the low walls separating the square paddies from each other and followed a zigzag pattern across the fields—fifty steps right, a ninety-degree turn left, fifty more steps, a right turn, fifty more steps, left, right, on and on.

Around noon we took our first rest beneath a few old, dry trees not far from a village. Two of the guards left, taking my empty bottle with them, and returned a few minutes later with a full bottle, which I drank gratefully. We resumed our journey, but instead of going to the village, we reversed our course and began a wide circle around it. About an hour later we stopped to rest again and to eat some rice. I sat on the ground, squinting to shield my eyes from the glaring sun.

Suddenly a shadow fell over me, screening out the harsh light, and I saw dark hair tumbling down over a black cotton dress. A bowl cupped in tiny hands was all I could make out at first. Then the woman knelt down, placed the bowl in front of me, and rose and left without a word. She was beautiful and I watched her diminutive figure grow smaller as she walked away. For one fleeting moment I wished she would return but the aroma of freshly cooked rice turned my thoughts from the woman to the food. The rice was all right but I really needed some meat or fish, since the meager diet was taking its toll on a body used to more protein.

The guards, especially Bastard, were gorging themselves with bananas which another villager had brought and my mouth watered for some of the fruit. I got Bastard's attention and pointed to a banana and then to myself, and in answer he let loose a burst from his automatic rifle. I was covered with flying dirt and sat there shaking with fear, sure that I was hit but discovering no blood. Suddenly my fear was gone, replaced by anger, and I could hardly stop myself from spitting toward him. When Bastard had opened up on me the other guards thought it was the beginning of an attack and they all jumped up, dropping their food on the ground and grabbing their guns. When they realized it was just Bastard harassing me, they all gave him dirty looks and cursed him for disturbing their meal. For once, I felt they were on my side. They retied my arms and then slung one end of the rope around my neck, pulling my head back. The rope was as rough as sandpaper and soon my neck was sore and raw. One of the guards picked up my leash and we went on our way. Judging from where I had been shot down and from the direction we had been traveling, I knew that we must be nearing Route 12, the road that the squadron had been bombing.

In the afternoon we arrived in an area that looked like some kind of camp, and as soon as we entered, forty or so guerrillas dressed in blue uniforms ran out to meet us. They laughed aloud, walking around me and hitting me on the head from behind. We had been there for about an hour when one of them had an idea, which they all seemed to agree with wholeheartedly.

They untied my arms, led me to some trees a short distance away, and tied me to one of them. At first I didn't mind this at all as I was happy to get away from the blue uniforms and their harassing, but when I saw them raise their weapons at me, I thought again my time had come. I yelled and screamed while they emptied their rifles into the tree and ground around me. As the bullets flew by my face they seemed to suck the air in with them, some of the slugs missing me by mere inches. I pressed my eyes closed, expecting one of the bullets to find its target. The firing stopped and I waited for a single, final bullet to hit me. Footsteps approached; the one who had had the idea in the first place came up to me, laughing. He laid the hot barrel of his M-1 on my neck, quickly pulled the rifle up next to my ear, and fired. A thousand little bells went off in my head and I vowed I would live through this to come back and find this man with the curly hair and purple scar under his eye.

Later, after the sun had gone down, I was untied from the

tree and my arms were trussed up again. We entered a cave at the base of the nearby mountain where the other guards had already assembled. They left me completely alone while they chatted with two girls from the nearby village. I lay back and dozed off, thinking of small cupped hands and Marina's blond hair.

I was awakened by the combined aromas of hot, steaming rice and rotten fish. When I opened my eyes I was greeted by an old woman with a kind smile who offered me a cup of rice covered with fish sauce. The rice was great but her smile nourished me as much, and I thanked her numerous times while she sat opposite me, following my every move. Since my hands were tied, I had to eat lying on my belly like an animal. Aside from the awful smell the fish was quite good and I could feel strength returning to my body. I wished I had a longer tongue as mine was too short to reach the bottom of the bowl. I motioned to her about my ropes, asking her without words to untie me. Silently she glanced toward the guards, who were not paying any attention to us, and then back to me. Our eyes met and for a moment I could see that she was debating with herself. Lowering her eyes, she slowly shook her head, obviously with regret, and I knew that she would have freed me if at all possible, so I nodded and smiled. She wiped out the bottom of the rice bowl with her fingers and put the remaining fish and rice into my mouth, then stood up and walked through the entrance of the cave. Her company had been soothing and now that she had left, I was totally depressed.

After the meal we continued our journey in the dark. In a few minutes we came to a small paved road and stopped at its edge. Route 12—I never thought that I would actually walk on it. The guards, motioning everyone to be quiet, scanned the sky carefully, as if half expecting to see airplanes swoop down on us. They waved us across the road. We started walking again, with the moon hanging heavily in the black frame of night, giving off a brilliant but ghostly light, and I wondered if it were shining as brightly at home. I heard the grinding of a truck in low gear far down the road. My feet were sore beyond words and the thought of traveling by truck was exhilarating. However, we turned and walked in the opposite direction from the sound and my hopes of riding quickly vanished. As we walked I constantly wished that a snake would bite one of them so that we could stop and I could sleep.

We came across a hut and a guard yelled something toward it. A voice from within answered and we proceeded to walk through the village. Once on the other side, we settled down for the night. I had barely put my head on the wet ground when I fell asleep. Dampness filtered through my clothes and I awoke, shivering, long before dawn. I listened to see if the guards were awake but they were warm and asleep under their blankets. I wondered whether the rifle blast had deafened my still-ringing ears.

In the morning we moved on without delay right after eating. Our new guide was very careful. He would not cross any clearings, no matter how small or well camouflaged, unless we all stopped and listened. We would then run across quickly and stop to listen again on the other side. I thought they were a bunch of idiots, but I was amused by their exaggerated caution. Whenever they were about to go across a clearing without stopping first, I would nod toward the sky and shake my head until they began to look for the nonexistent plane.

We arrived at a neatly kept community. The people, mostly women dressed in blue knit sweater shirts, quickly formed a semicircle as we approached and quietly watched us come into the village. The old women were bare-breasted—an ugly sight with their bosoms hanging in droopy folds. All of them were chewing betel nuts and spitting streams of red juice through their corroded teeth. Children with distended bellies hung onto their mothers' skirts and curiously watched the armed men and their captive.

We stopped in front of the assembled crowd and I was ordered to sit down. Whenever I moved or shifted my position, the entire crowd cautiously stepped backwards. A few huts were standing next to a cave that seemed large enough to house at least fifteen families. These huts were only frames with a roof and no walls, the floors built about a foot off the ground to keep the moisture out. A woman was weaving a beautiful, multicolored mat in one of the huts and it seemed amazing that she could make such a beautiful thing with the crude, crooked loom she had to use.

Though no opportunity for escape had yet presented itself, the thought of escape was always on my mind, especially with aircraft continuously overhead. All I really needed to signal them was a mirror. I tried again in this village to get one, by talking in gestures to the women, holding my hands in front of my face and making a pulling motion on my beard, which had already grown coarse and thick. I was trying to tell them that I wanted a shave and, of course, hoped they might bring me a mirror. Usually the women shook their heads. When I made my gestures here, a young woman watching me vigorously nodded her head. She ran off toward the cave, went inside and quickly reappeared. She looked up at the sky to be sure no aircraft was in sight and then produced a mirror from her black skirt. She wouldn't let go of the mirror, only letting me straighten it to look at myself. I couldn't believe my eyes. My face was a mass of pus-filled cuts and the rope had worn a deep blue welt in my neck. She quickly took the mirror back and after pointing to the sky and making sounds like a machine gun, hid it under her skirt. I took out my pills to swap with her but she shook her head and walked off. I called after her, taking off my shoes to try a new trade, but the guard I had named Thief, now serving as a permanent guard along with Tan and Bastard, ran over screaming and brutally snatched the mirror away from her. He held it over his head as if he were going to smash it on the ground, pointed at her and then at me. Finally, he gave it back to her and she quickly fled. Most of my female audience had walked away to get back to whatever they were doing before we came. Two women nearby were mashing rice in a hollowed-out tree stump, using six-foot-long poles with grips cut into them at the midpoint. As one woman pulled up, the other smashed down with tremendous force, making a thumping sound that alternately rose and fell.

I was led over to the entrance of a cave and shoved inside. They tied me loosely to a platform built off the floor and then left me alone. I wiggled myself free of the ropes and the guard sitting about twenty feet away eyed me casually and then looked away, as if he didn't mind. I then hung my shoes and socks to dry on a nearby bamboo pole. The guards were squatting in their typical Asian way. A few villagers had joined them and all were smoking their small bamboo pipes. I could see the profile of Bastard—his black hair sticking out as if he had just been struck by lightning. He would look my way every so often and then continue talking, shifting his weight from one bare foot to the other. Thief crouched next to him, rocking slightly on his green sneakers. The shadows filtering in through the cave hinted at the coming night. More villagers began coming into the cave.

A small, full-breasted woman sat down close to me, smiling. In her arms she carried a child wrapped in one of those gaily colored cloths. A bowlegged young man knelt down next to her and, nodding his head, he stretched out his hand to me. We shook hands and I felt the much-needed warmth of friendship in his grasp. I then motioned with my arms to ask if I could hold the baby, whereupon the woman looked at the man with approval and hesitatingly gave her child to me. Carefully I took the child in my arms, supporting its head with my hand. Some of the villagers moaned and their faces took on a frightened look. The baby was so soft and warm. I felt that it was the only friend I had. I smiled reassuringly at the mother and gently gave the baby back. Though she smiled, too, I could see that she was relieved. The Laotians are so superstitious about ghosts entering their children that when a baby is born, they often squeeze its head out of shape or mutilate it by notching an ear so that the child will be too ugly for any ghost to want it.

The baby broke the spell in the cave and other mothers came forward, holding their babies out toward me. One mother tried to hand me her son but he hung onto her skirt frantically, crying from sheer fright. I took the St. Christopher medal I was wearing and hung it around the child's neck. His crying stopped immediately; wide-eyed, he fingered the medal like some newly found plaything. The child's happiness put the people more at ease and for a little while I forgot that I was a prisoner and was almost happy. We communicated with hands and gestures and laughed at our misinterpretations, their weathered, rawhide faces crinkling into a million creases, exposing small, yellow-red teeth. Bent and leathery, an old woman shrouded in black, her graying hair coiled into a small wispy knot at the back of her head, moved silently over to me with a little boy and girl grasping her hands. Hesitatingly, she pointed to the children, then to me. At first I did not understand but realized a second later that she was asking if I had any children. Even though I did not, I slowly nodded my head. She pointed to the boy's lower naked part and then to the girl's and then back to me. I pointed to the little girl, holding up three fingers, wondering whether Marina would prefer three boys, three girls, or a mixed bag. "*Uuh, Uuh,*" the woman replied, hugging the children close. Pointing to my ring and then to a young woman nearby who immediately stepped back at the gesture, she said, *Pusaul,* meaning girl in Laotian, and I rubbed my eyes with my hands, as if crying. The old woman seemed on the verge of crying herself. Gathering up her children, she left, looking back once and shaking her head sorrowfully. The knowledge that someone here actually cared about me gave me a warm feeling inside. I lay back against the wall of the cave and dozed off.

When I awoke, the guards were up and putting on their rucksacks. I regretted that we had to leave and reluctantly put on my still wet socks and shoes. Oddly enough, we didn't leave immediately. I was brought a ball of cold rice and a bowl with a red-green thick sauce. Not realizing it was hot peppers, I bit into a mouthful of sauce-covered rice and swallowed. Tears swelled in my eyes and my head felt as if it were exploding. My mouth was so numb I couldn't utter a sound. I tried to drink water and eat rice to stop the pain but the torch in my mouth and ears burned on. I pressed the ball of the remaining rice into a flat cake and stuck it into my jacket pocket. The guards trussed up my arms loosely and we left.

The sun was beating down by now and we were walking in

an oven. The heat rising from the ground made mirage after mirage, until the distance seemed a wavy pattern of lakes. I wanted to take off my jacket and shirt but the ropes were tied over them and there was no stopping the group now. My thin nylon bag was wrapped around my waist like their loincloth and they accepted it as such. My water bottle, held around my neck by the mosquito netting I had torn out of the bag, clinked against the zipper of my jacket. I had filled it with crystal clear water at the village and like magic the iodine tablets had separated a third of the water into a thick precipitate. No wonder I had dysentery.

I discovered that my comb was missing. I remembered that Thief had wanted my jacket to show to some villagers and when at first I refused, he had picked up his rifle, forcing me to agree. Now I was sure he had the comb. "You thief, you lousy thief!" I shouted, looking at the ground. A simple ten-cent comb just did not exist here and was a priceless item to me, one of the few things I still possessed. The loss of the comb bothered me the rest of the day and evening. I felt like doing Thief in and whenever I looked at him, he avoided my eyes and looked away, a sure sign that he had stolen it.

We were approaching another village, which meant a chance to rest or maybe even the end of our journey. The usual warning device—a two-foot-long bamboo section with a stick inserted in it—hung from a limb a few hundred feet from the village. As always, a guard banged the bamboo with its stick slowly, gradually hitting faster and faster until he was hitting it as fast as he could. Most of the time the headman came out to greet us and to take us in. This time, however, villagers approached us from all sides and when Bastard yelled something to them, they raised their weapons. The headman stepped out from the group and waved us away with frantic motions of his arm. Even after the quieter of the two brothers tried to hand him a chicken he had stolen on the way out of the last village, the headman made it obvious that there was to be no food for us.

My guards did not like to be told what to do—they were young, none older than twenty, the youngest one about thirteen. We started to walk toward the village without the headman's permission but they must have expected it. They fired a warning shot toward us and my guards realized it could mean a shoot-out. Being outnumbered, they decided against risking it.

As we walked on, I studied my captors. The two brothers had on light khaki uniforms, badly worn and frayed, and both wore sandals cut from tires. Every evening they smoked waterpipes which they often carved while walking. In order to smoke, they placed a little black ball of opium in the bowl and lit it. Two or three drags and they would be on a trip. They both carried backpacks filled with ammunition and old hand grenades.

Their weapons were as old as the grenades—Chinese rifles fitted with a detachable, needle-sharp bayonet. Bastard's weapon was a Russian automatic with a drum magazine attached underneath. He treated the gun badly and used it for just about everything—moving logs, pushing over rocks, and stirring fires and soups. Thief carried a U.S. carbine and an ammunition belt around his waist that read "U.S. Cal 30."

We made a wide circle around the next village. The guards were carrying their rifles, the butts resting on their hips, ready for action. I had to laugh to myself because they didn't know how foolish they looked. The way they were lined up, one man with an automatic weapon could have wiped them all out. But it suddenly occurred to me that any danger to the guards was a danger to me, too.

Unbelievable as it might sound, the guards and I had somehow grown a little closer, evidently because I didn't give them any trouble. I hoped they would relax so I could make my getaway and it seemed to be working. The rope was put on very loosely at times, to the point where it actually fell off my arms, and I would immediately put it back just the way it had been, while the guards nodded their approval. They would even go so far as to throw the loose end of the rope over my shoulder when the jungle trails got too overgrown. "What a lazy bunch," I chuckled to myself. "This will be your downfall." Only Bastard, whenever he got a chance, would harass me out of pure hatred.

"*Bie, bie!*" Bastard suddenly pointed his rifle in the direction of a well-built hut and began yelling. He picked up my rope as he ran by me, pulling me sideways, and the closer we got to the hut, the more he yelled. Faster and faster he ran until I finally started to fall. I tried to catch myself by running faster and I hit the grass hut and crashed through its wall, with only my legs remaining outside. Tan and Thief yanked me out and an angry man jumped out of the hut, wondering what was going on. He came running my way and I nodded toward the guard holding my rope, indicating that it wasn't my fault. He began yelling at the guard and pointed to the large hole in his hut, splattered with blood from my mashed nose. "Damn you, Bastard, you son of a bitch," I yelled. I walked toward him, seething inside, and he backed away, jerking the rope. A shot stopped me in my tracks and he started to laugh, thinking it all a good joke.

Beyond Bastard, an entire guerrilla patrol marched into view. One man from the patrol came over to me, took off my rope, and led me up to a hut. Before we went into the hut, I saw several more soldiers emerging from a cave so well concealed that I wouldn't have known it was there had I not looked directly at it. The hut was almost completely dark inside. Once my eyes became adjusted to the dim light, I saw five soldiers sitting in the far corner, reading something by candlelight. They paid absolutely no attention to me. Exhausted, I lay down next to the wall. Lying on my side, my arms still tied behind me, I rotated from side to side occasionally so my arms would not go to sleep. I thought of home, of my buddies on the carrier, and about my chances of getting out of this alive. Through the smokehole in the roof the sky appeared deep purple and black with heavy rain clouds. Rain always made me feel serene and I hoped for it now. I lay motionless and the rain began to hit the Kaa leaves of the roof, putting me to sleep.

I awoke soon. The men were still reading. What luck it would be if we could rest here another day. I couldn't last much longer on rice and water without some meat or fruit. Tears of depression clouded my eyes as I wondered what lay ahead. I also wondered who would get my $10,000 life insurance policy that two other pilots and I had made out on the carrier, each of us naming the other two as beneficiaries. Were they still alive? How long would it take for the news of my death to reach those at home? Would I be thrown in the bush and forgotten? Should I have made out a will? Not that I had very much to leave, but what I did have meant a lot to me. I tried to think of pleasant things to chase away the depression and when that failed, I prayed.

Emerging from a dream, I was face to face with a soldier who was kneeling next to me and putting something like Merthiolate on my nose and lip. He had also brought a bowl of steaming rice, fish, and three bananas. This fantastic dinner gave me much strength. I could think more clearly now and my thoughts became brighter.

Loud yelling and screaming ruptured the quiet in the pitch-black hut. An ear-splitting explosion nearby went clear through my bones. "Bombs!" I thought. I was up, bumping and running with the others, falling off the ladder halfway down. The night burst into brilliant daylight for a split second and more explosions thundered all around. How I made it with the others into the cave I had noticed earlier, I don't know, but instantly I realized that I had blown a chance of getting away. Now the cave was full of people. Bombs continued to explode, and I wondered if I was in Vietnam. It seemed ridiculous to have been nearly killed by my own people. The first bomb went off not more than a quarter of a mile away and had it hit a little closer, it would have been the end for us. I was now on the receiving end and didn't like it a bit. I was also still furious with myself for letting such an opportunity to escape slip away.

Squatting, we made our way deeper into the cave. The ceiling became lower and I had to crouch down while the Laotians could still stand upright. At first I couldn't see the fire burning way back in the cave, but the smoke creeping along the sloped ceiling made my eyes smart. This was the first time I felt that there was little difference between prisoner and captors. My rope was off and I was squatting among them with the tiny fire warming our hands. Nobody blamed me for the bombing. I was a helpless victim just as they were. I would have liked to sit down but the ground was ankle-deep in mud, reminding me that my shoes were still in the hut. I hoped if the hut were still standing, there would be time to get them in the morning. I accepted the small pipe a man on my right offered me, making me cough and them laugh. I yearned for a bed or even just a dry floor.

Someone was sleeping next to me on a bamboo mat when I awoke the following morning. We had snuggled close to each other to keep warm during the night and unexpectedly somebody had thrown a blanket over us. It felt so good to be warm that I didn't dare move, for fear of waking the man and losing the blanket. A few minutes later, however, my friend and some of the others woke up and he rolled up the blanket and disappeared through the cave entrance. From where we had slept to ten feet from the entrance, the ground was dry. Looking out the opening, either the sun had not yet risen or it was overcast. I hoped for more rain, which might mean a day of rest, and then happily realized that it had begun to drizzle.

Breakfast was nourishing and tasty—warm rice, meat of some kind, and two bananas, one of which I ate and the other I saved in my jacket pocket.

My shoes were brought in, as well as my filled water bottle, making it apparent we would be moving on, so my hope of remaining there the rest of the day dwindled appreciably. I decided to try walking barefoot, thinking the mud might be good for my sore feet. The guards appeared at the entrance, wearing transparent red plastic sheets, and yelled at me to come out. I stepped out in the now pounding rain and was soaking wet almost immediately. Puddles of rainwater had collected in the huge elephant leaves and I funneled the clean, fresh water into my mouth, drinking myself full, and then quickly rubbed and washed myself. My nose made my hands bloody and I was afraid the wound had opened up again, but it was only the scab dissolving in the rain.

I felt good and clean and there were no ropes, my arms free and useful again. Soon, however, I started to shiver in the cold and wished that my nylon sleeping bag was waterproof, but the rain gave me such comfort that I dismissed the cold, the wet bag, and wet clothes. It may have given me emotional soothing, but physically it soon became a torment.

Scorpions, little crabs, and leeches were everywhere, adding to my misery, and as we walked I noticed blood running down my ankles. At first I didn't pay any attention to it but when I pulled up my trousers, even the guards who were used to such things, were amazed when they saw the black leeches girding my ankles. It was a sickening sight—a hundred of them clinging to each ankle, blood running down as if from a wound. I tried to pull them off but got nowhere since, as soon as a leech was free from my ankle, it stuck to my fingers, and their slimy skins made it just about impossible to get a good grip on them. One of the guards came to my aid, setting to work on the leeches with a cut bamboo stick, scraping them off and flinging them away with a flick of his wrist. As we resumed our march I saw the leeches wriggling on the trail, trying to find something else to which they could become attached. They would gorge themselves with blood and then drop off, leaving their victim bleeding from the tiny wound. The real problem was that the saliva of the leeches prevented the blood from coagulating and after the leech had dropped away, the sore wouldn't stop bleeding. A mixture of blood and water poured out from under my trousers. I wasn't the only one, as some of the guards had bleeding legs as well.

We didn't make much headway. The water in some areas was so deep that it was impossible to ford and the trails were very slippery. We could make it up a slight hill only by grabbing exposed roots along the trail and pulling ourselves up. I was lucky to have my shoes now, since their corrugated rubber soles made traveling easier.

Around 10:00 A.M. the rain stopped and patches of blue appeared in the sky, allowing the sun's rays to hit the earth. The rain disappeared almost as if it had never started and our clothes were dry within half an hour. Soon the jungle began to steam and come alive with birds and insects. We came across a recently bombed-out village, approached it cautiously, and then sprinted away as if we were being chased. At first I didn't see any sense in this mad dash, but then I remembered that bombers would also drop delayed-fuse bombs mixed with their conventional load.

We left the flat country with its checkered rice paddies and entered the karst* mountain area. Previously, we had had to climb a couple of hills each day but now it seemed that we were traveling up and down continuously. The limestone mountains were steep and jagged and when traveling in the narrow canyons between them, I could sometimes touch both sides. When I looked up, the walls seemed to meet, many feet above me in the sky.

The trail took us along a red, muddy river toward a ridge. I couldn't imagine where we were going, climbing over rocks with razor-sharp edges. Up one mountain, then down, alongside nearly vertical cliffs. One slip could send one down the rocky blades below to be split open like a watermelon.

We climbed down to a river, which seemed like the same one we had paralleled earlier. How we were to cross this river was a mystery to me. The trail had been washed out by the water runoff that had cut deep gullies in the bank. Then I saw a makeshift rowboat and wondered in dismay how they would take it across the river without capsizing. They loaded most of their gear, tied it down, and three of the guards got in while two others held the flimsy craft. The two then jumped in and pushed themselves out with long bamboo poles and, in somewhat calmer waters, they began rowing. I could see the boat starting to spin around, out of control. The men with me stood up, yelling as if they could do something about it, but the boat had already capsized. "Hope all you bastards drown," I yelled out at them, knowing that they wouldn't understand. I prayed that they wouldn't make it, especially Bastard. As it turned out, they all got to the other side, dragging the boat behind them.

A villager rowed back to pick up the rest of us but I refused to go because my arms were tied and I would not be able to swim. "No, no!" I shook my head and kept motioning to my arms. The rope was taken off, only to be retied—and now it

---

*A limestone plateau marked by sinks or karst holes, interspersed with abrupt ridges and irregular protuberant rocks, and by caverns and underground streams.

was also around my neck, pulling my head so far back it was choking me. Into the craft I went, trussed like a pig bound for the market. Those who had already crossed were standing on the other side, their rifles aimed at me—as if I would be crazy enough to try to escape by jumping in the river. If we capsized I knew I would somehow have to hold onto the boat. I was sure that the guards would be too busy trying to save their own necks for them to give me a hand. Luckily we made it to the other side, arriving a few hundred yards downstream from where the others had landed. I was marched away with the rope left on me just as it had been for the crossing.

Hours later we entered a village and the guards loosened my ropes, which I slid off with no one objecting. My neck had been pulled painfully backwards and I was sure that it was permanently damaged. Whenever I had moved my head forward or put my arms down, the rope had cut into my throat, and now I couldn't utter a sound.

For the past few hours I had seen mostly sky and my eyes were burning. But I could see that the village was a truly beautiful place. The trees were dark green and full, like open umbrellas. Neat fences surrounded well-kept huts, a temple, and a pasture area where some white cows and a tan horse were grazing. The entire place reminded me of Disneyland. The guards started picking fruit and motioned for me to do the same. Sometimes I just couldn't figure them out.

A few minutes after our arrival three monks came our way. Their heads were shaven clean and they were wrapped in yellow-orange cloth. Two of them wore the loose end of their garments flung over their shoulders, while the third was naked from the waist up. They greeted us and the guards exchanged a few words with two of them. The third one came to me and gave me what looked like a large peapod, six inches long. Within the pod were numerous rock-hard brown beans, which I had seen the women wear for necklaces. These beans lay in a gelatinous material that tasted like delicious jam. After seeing how much I liked them, the monk and I walked over to a tree where many more of them lay on the ground. He motioned for me to join him and I dove to the ground, collecting and sucking on them. The monk shook his head and rubbed his stomach to let me know that too many were not good, but I had not eaten anything so delicious for a long time and I wasn't going to let a chance like this pass.

Actually this village was as deserted as so many we had seen. The villagers had taken shelter in the surrounding hills and caves because of the constant threat of air strikes. The monks were not from this village, but custom allowed them to enter huts and take what they needed. Everyone, including the monks, filled his pockets with whatever he could get and I grabbed more beans until my pockets were bulging. I took off my bag to put some beans into it but then quickly rewrapped my "loincloth" so as not to give the others an idea. That would have been the last I would see of that priceless but unnoticeable piece of cloth.

We left in a hurry and walked without stopping until the sun had only a few minutes left before disappearing behind the mountains. Then we stopped. The guards ate but didn't feed me, evidently thinking I had had enough food in the form of the jam-covered beans. They finished their meal, then settled down for the night, even though the sun was just barely down. These were early-to-bed-and-early-to-rise people, unless they had to do otherwise. In the morning the guards were nearly always up before me but they would let me sleep until I woke of my own accord—never later than 5:30 or 6:00 A.M. The first light of dawn got them up to make a fire, and the villagers went to their local waterhole to wash their rice. Once the pot was on the fire, everybody relaxed.

In the morning, without my asking, I was motioned toward the bush and two guards followed me at a safe distance. Then I had my daily ration of rice with some fish sauce over it. It was a slow morning and I was eager to get going since I felt every day would bring me closer to someone who could speak English. I felt terribly lonely. Even if the end of the journey meant prison, at least I would have someone with whom to share my misery.

I anxiously got up and shouted, *"Bie, bie!"* to get them going, but they just sat there, one of them plucking a live chicken.

While sitting there waiting I inspected myself, especially my feet. They were black with bruises and yellow with pus-filled pockets of infection and the toenail on my right big toe was just about off. Something round was lying in my left shoe, and it turned out to be a bull leech, bloated full of my blood. I squeezed it between my fingers and a very thin stream of blood a couple of feet long squirted from it. I squashed the leech on a rock, taking pleasure in the large red stain it left, but quickly wished I hadn't done it. Perhaps this rock in the middle of the village was holy and the red stain would be some kind of a sacrilege.

I had already been in trouble because of Laotian taboos and superstitions. The day before, a villager had given me some bananas and I had taken them with my left hand, whereupon he pulled out his machete, mumbled, *"Cha ka chao,"* and laid the blade against his throat to show me that my head was going to come off. The commotion brought Thief over. He pushed the villager away and must have explained that as a foreigner I didn't understand (though I did eventually) what an insult it was to accept anything with one's left hand.

We finally left. I noticed the plucked chicken, still alive, hanging by its feet from the guard's belt. The chicken was worse off than I—at least I wouldn't be boiled for dinner at the end of the day.

Fortunately, they set a slow pace, as if they wanted to lose some time. My feet were giving me trouble and with every step I had to stifle a groan. When we stopped to rest, I dissolved two iodine tablets in a handful of water and rubbed my feet with the solution. At first there was no real sensation but then my feet began to sting. Finally they burned so much I had to wash them off with spit and water until the pain was at least tolerable. I was certain that any infection was literally burned out.

As we walked, I spotted something that gave me a sudden surge of hope; Bastard's tobacco box had a small built-in mirror. If I could get the mirror I would have a real chance of being rescued, once I had successfully escaped. With all the aircraft flying around, it would be a cinch to attract a pilot's attention and get picked up. The more I thought about the mirror, the stronger I felt about escaping. I tried to find out again how much longer it would be before we reached our destination. Pointing first to the sun, then to the eastern horizon, I described an arc overhead toward the west. "One day—two days?" I asked, counting out the numbers with my fingers. The guards didn't answer; instead they loosened my ropes and acted more kindly and pleasantly than ever before. It seemed very odd and I began to worry about what was to come.

4 INTERROGATION

"Comment ca va?" I stared unbelievingly at the man who spoke these words. Bowing before me, then shaking my hand, was a rather short chubby man wearing a light jacket, black boots, and black-rimmed glasses. For all I knew, he could have been anyone walking down a street in San Francisco—he looked quite Caucasian—and I wondered where he came from. As soon as I was over the shock of hearing French spoken, I grabbed his hand and shook it violently, saying, *"Comment ca va"* myself. My happiness at finding someone I could talk with had no end.

He warmly put his arm around my shoulder and together we walked toward a rock overhang so huge that a three-story building could have fitted easily under it. Steps cut into the rock led to the area sheltered by the overhang and after we had slowly climbed up, I was told I could sit down if I wished. A tall, handsome man, burned dark brown by the sun, climbed up after us. He also shook my hand, asking me in French how I was.

"Good!" I told him. "It is so good to talk to someone, so very good." I wished I had studied my French better when I was in school, for now was the time to use it. I had a thousand questions but the really important one was, "What's going to be done with me?" The tall man, who was dressed in a blue shirt and blue trousers, had carried up a bundle of books bound together with a piece of string. He sat down next to me. *"Qu'est-ce que vous appelez-vous?"* he asked. "Dieter," I answered, *"mon nom est* Dieter Dengler." They repeated my name several times, then told me theirs, which I found impossible to pronounce.

These two looked so civilized and out of place. I wondered if there might be some other American prisoners here, but the only people I could see were villagers and their children.

My guards came up the steps and sat down beside us, smiling and nodding constantly while the shorter man, who turned out to be the province chief, kept talking to them, removing his glasses every now and then. I gave the guards a dirty look and pointed to the marks the rope had left on my neck. I took off my shoes and showed him my feet, pointing to Bastard, who was responsible for all the maltreatment I had received. At once the province chief summoned a soldier, who brought a leather carrying case containing medical supplies. The soldier dipped a Q-Tip into a thin Merthiolate solution and began painting my feet with it. I wondered how, in the middle of this jungle, they had ever obtained Q-Tips.

The province chief wanted to know how old I was and I told him, "Twenty-eight, and you?" He told me he was forty-two or fifty-two, I wasn't sure which.

"You have an accent. Where are you from?" he asked. "*Allemagne*, Germany, *Deutschland*," I answered. His mouth dropped open in surprise and he pointed a finger at me. "*Allemagne*, I have been in Germany and Geneva. I have been in Zurich, I have been in Paris, I have been in Dusseldorf, I have been in Stuttgart, I have . . ."

I interrupted him excitedly. "Stuttgart—that's where I am from!" Actually Calw was about twenty-five miles outside of Stuttgart, but that was close enough for me. We fiercely shook hands again, with that special warmth between people who meet in some distant place and who share a link in the past. "Do you know where the train station is—and Koenigstrasse?" I wanted to know.

"Yes, yes, I bought some cloth there." He went on to describe the street in all the detail that only someone who had actually been there could possibly know.

At times I was confused and did not understand him because of my poor French, but by repeating and gesturing with our hands we got our point across. I felt I had a friend. He asked me how I felt and I told him I felt all right, but that I sure could go for a meal of something other than rice. I complained to him about the way the guards had treated me, whereupon he scolded them and they nodded their heads but didn't answer back. There was no doubt that this man was in charge. I had worried about what might become of me now that the journey was over, but it seemed that in the hands of such a genuinely good man, I would be well treated.

Gently, he began talking again. "Your poor mother, how worried she must be. She probably knows that you have been shot down and wonders if you are dead. Since we are friends and since you are German, I will let you write a couple of letters—one to your mother and one to your wife."

"I am not married, but I have a fiancée whom I am going to marry as soon as I get back," I answered, hoping he would still approve the letter.

"Fine, fine," he said, and he called out an order in Laotian. Then he promised that he, too, would write a letter to my mother to tell her that I was alive and well.

A few minutes later an old woman arrived and handed the province chief a small, blue notebook. He thanked her silently by nodding his head. He ripped out a few pages and gave them to me. It was of poor grade, like the paper we used in Germany during the war, but it was the first paper I had seen since I was shot down. The guards eyed the paper enviously since paper for cigarettes was a real luxury to them and the leaves they had to use were a pretty poor substitute. I indicated that I didn't have anything to write with and he took a pen from his shirt pocket—a fat, gray fountain pen like the ones found in the States. "American!" I blurted out in surprise. He shook his finger and kept repeating, *"Chine, Chine."*

The last page of the notebook was printed in English, a table of measurements in the troy and metric systems. It is hard to describe the wave of emotion that swept over me. I had been cut off so completely from friends and from all that was familiar, that even the tiniest reminder of how things had been, choked me up. "American, American," I half mumbled in awe, pointing to a "gallon," a "pint," and so on down the column.

"No, no, Chinese!" was the chief's reply. At the bottom of

the page, printed in small letters, were the words, "Made in China." The pen carried the same trademark. "I don't give a damn who said the Chinese made this stuff," I thought to myself, "I know it's not made in China."

I began wondering about what I should put in the letter to my mother. When my father was lost in action it was a long time before my mother actually found out that he had died. "Missing in action" was all she had to live on during that time of waiting and I remember how not knowing anything for certain, one way or another, tore at her. I didn't want this to happen again—not to my mother or to Marina—and it was also important to me to let the outside world know I was still alive.

The province chief said something about taking a picture and left, to return shortly with a German Voightlaender Vito-B camera.

"A German camera," I said, surprised again. "Chinese," he answered, but this I knew for sure to be German. He wanted to take my picture, but at first I frowned and shook my head. I could just see my picture tagged to a fictitious political statement attributed to me, appearing on the front pages of the newspapers in Hanoi, Peking, or in the West. "But then," I thought, "here is a friend. He has eaten my native food and slept in my homeland and wouldn't pull anything like that, especially after saying he would write a letter to my mother, too." I agreed to the photograph but not with the loosely hanging ropes on my arms, so he ordered them removed. I wanted that picture to get home and I knew that if I seemed to be in bad shape, the Communists would probably never release it. I needed a comb and this was the time to get even with Thief, so I told the province chief that Thief had taken my comb. He told Thief to give it back. Thief spread his arms and shook his head, as if he didn't have it. I knew better and pointed to the pocket where I thought he carried it. After a moment of motionless silence, Thief grudgingly handed me my comb. Triumph is sweet and I couldn't suppress the big grin spreading across my face.

My hair was so full of mud, sap, and bugs that I couldn't comb it out. I did the best I could, smiled, and the province chief shot a couple of pictures. I thought it was definitely too dark to take pictures and started to ask him about that. Again he said, "Chinese," and I guessed he was talking about the film.

I wrote two letters, one to my mother and one to Marina. There was so much to say, yet I didn't want to make a mistake and write something that could be cut out and printed in some propaganda sheet along with my name. I wrote the letter to my mother in German and printed the letter to Marina, leaving no space where words not my own could be inserted. I wanted to say something about what I had gone through but decided against it, because I was sure that that would keep the letters from reaching home. My mother and Marina both knew I hated rice but I wrote that "I had all the rice I wanted, a real feast for me since I loved rice so much." Actually, I had learned to like rice by then and respected it, because no other food by itself could have kept me alive. The low-grade paper soaked up ink like a blotter, making the words grow big and fuzzy.

As I was writing, the province chief and I talked about Germany and how I had gotten to the U.S.A. He became increasingly agitated. "How could you fall for the American trick? It was they who killed your father and leveled your towns, and now you are just about giving your life for them."

"I am a pilot. I have a job to do and I do it when I'm told. When I joined the navy there was no war in sight, but now there is, and I'm obligated to it."

He went on and on, and surprisingly enough he didn't get too angry. I hoped and prayed, however, that no aircraft would fly over because that really would have set things off.

I finally finished the letters, after nearly an hour and a half of talking and writing, but didn't sign them. Instead, I printed my name at the bottom since I didn't want to give a forger anything to copy.

For dinner I was given two small eggs and some sugar with the rice. I was happy and couldn't help thinking what a wonderful man the province chief was. While I ate, he shifted in place and bent slightly toward me, his two hands clasped in his lap, and quietly said, "You will be released in two weeks but you must promise me that you will go back to Germany."

His announcement was so sudden and so unexpected that it

knocked me speechless for a second. Nodding rapidly, despite the pain in my neck, I tried to tell him in my broken French that he could bet his life on that. What I didn't tell him was that my tour of duty with the navy was not finished and they would hold me to it. "As soon as I'm out, I'll go back to Germany, and right now you are invited also to come and stay with my family. There's lots of room."

The province chief thanked me for my invitation. He handed me a couple of blue envelopes for the letters, telling me not to seal the envelopes because his superiors would want to read the letters. I never once doubted that they would be read and the fact that he confided it to me again meant he was on my side. Maybe he was even telling me the truth about my release.

I had used only two pages for my letters and the rest I stuck in my jacket. "Where am I going from here?" I asked him.

"You will be kept with seven other Americans until you are released."

I was overjoyed to think I'd be with people who spoke English. "Where are they now?"

"Oh, about one and a half day's walk from here." Then he asked, "Do you have any money?"

I thought it better not to tell him of the $200 still in my shoes and showed him only the thirteen dollars still in my wallet.

"Do you want to change it into Laotian money? We can change it for *kip*, Laotian currency."

This proved he had to be my friend. An enemy would have just taken the money, not offered to change it.

The province chief continued, "In the camp where you will be going, you can use these kips to trade with the guards for toothpaste, chickens, paper, and things of that nature."

This was too good to be true. "Fine, fine," I said, giving him the thirteen dollars. Probably the other prisoners would have run out of money by now and we could have a feast. Once I was released, if it was before their release, I would leave them my $200 to tide them over until they, too, got out.

The province chief figured out the amount I would get in

exchange. He explained the exchange rate between the currencies and computed the total due me. He counted out the kips very slowly and the wad of money in my hand was about an inch thick. I wondered whether he had been as good to the others before me or whether he was treating me well only because he thought me to be German.

I folded the money and put it into my pocket, along with the leftover sugar that I had carefully wrapped in a piece of paper. The guards watched me with envy. A few minutes later one of the guards brought us a couple of cabangs (jungle candles made out of tree pitch and wrapped in leaves), which gave off more smoke than light. A villager with a beautiful voice began to sing. Tears of happiness streamed down my cheeks—it was so good to be with someone who was on my side. We talked some more, but nothing further was said about the military.

"How many people are there in the Congress?" he queried. I didn't know. "How many in the Senate?" Again I didn't know. It was embarrassing, especially since he translated everything to the villagers and guards sitting around us. I hoped he was telling them exactly what I was saying and not adding his own to it. One question he repeated for my benefit, before he translated it to the people, was, "If you don't even know your own government, how could you possibly understand about ours?" The people around us nodded, some smiling, others looking at me sourly.

While we were sitting there a young man dressed all in black arrived and, bowing low, shook my hand and introduced himself as the province chief's son. The two of them continued asking me questions and I somehow felt uneasy.

"There will be a party given in your honor tonight!" the son said. Everyone nodded happily after this was translated. Warm water was brought up and an old woman and man helped me wash, and again something like Merthiolate was put on my cut-up body. When I was clean and had eaten some rice I fell asleep, totally exhausted.

The province chief's son shook me awake in the morning and told me he had to leave on patrol. The chief himself arrived at about 11:00 A.M. He was very jovial, shaking my hand. The sun was out and everything looked great. He offered me a cigarette, saying, "Chinese." I told him about ten times that I didn't smoke but he kept insisting, waving the pack before me. We talked, and on a few occasions we both were just short of yelling at each other, especially when I was accused of bombing women and children. In fact, I was told to sign a statement denouncing the bombings. "We understand that you are a soldier, but now that you are here, you don't have to be ashamed at all to say what you really feel inside, that you don't want war. Haven't you had enough? Your mother lost her husband because of the Americans and now you cause her—no, the U.S. causes her so much grief. Stay here with us, don't go back to the war." He went on and on.

"In your home, the U.S., they shoot one another. Just open your paper and you will know what I am talking about. Most people are against the war, which is proven by the many antiwar rallies." He was up-to-date and with no effort he told me dates and places of antiwar rallies and named the universities. He also talked about the problem of the black man who, he said, was welcome in Laos but not in the U.S. "You want to show us a better way of life, and yet you can't even solve your own problems."

There was little I could say to all that and I was no match for him at dates, names, and places.

"Your own government—your people are a mass of uninformed individuals. There are always two sides and now you sit here and eat our food and you don't even want to listen to our side." Then he said how awful it was that President Kennedy was killed by one of his own fellow citizens. He leaned forward, his face close to mine, and in a soft but demanding voice said, "It is something to be proud of, not ashamed of, to be honest and stand by yourself and tell the truth."

All the time the guards just sat there, not knowing what we were saying, but seeing and hearing the heated statements. They had fixed their bayonets to their rifles, something they had not done before.

"You can live in China. I'll tell you what I'll do, we'll walk to Hanoi; we'll take you to Peking; we'll not teach you with words, you can go and look for yourself. Of course, we can't fly you there, we are not rich like the U.S. We'd like to drive you, but you know that your own aircraft will bomb us, so you will have to walk. You'll eat and sleep with our people and you will find that they are good and that they are not here to harm anyone." Again he gave me the paper to sign, but I shook my head.

The province chief talked to the guards for a while and then left. It became apparent we were all leaving, and looking at the guards, I knew something was up. Thief shook his fists at me.

We left in a rush. The guards grabbed me and ran me for about half an hour. Suddenly they stopped and threw me to the ground. I tried to fight back, but it only made them rougher and more furious. They tied a rope around my ankles, passed the end of it over a limb, and hauled me up until I hung head downward. They then set to beating me with their rifles and sticks. I saw stars, became unconscious, came back, saw more stars, and then only came to when the guards poured a bucket of water over me. All I could make out were blurry feet and legs, some of them kicking dirt. I was then grabbed from behind by my hair and pulled nearly to eye level with a soldier's face, as I gasped for air against the blood and fluid that ran up my throat and out of my mouth. The beating started again and I was knocked out by a sharp blow from behind. I don't know how long they continued, but when I came to I had been cut down and was lying in a pool of red, sticky mud. At first I thought I was dead, but then a sharp pain flashed through my body somewhere and I quickly closed my eyes, hoping no one had seen that I was conscious. A sharp kick in the back made me cry out in pain, and water was poured over me again. I could see better now because the blood was running down my face instead of up into my eyes. "Got to swallow that blood," I thought, "can't afford to lose any of it if I ever want to make it home."

I hoped for aircraft; I hoped for Norm, Spook, and the rest of the gang with their Skyraiders and their 20-mm cannons, to kill us all, everybody, and scrape this place off the map.

The villagers then brought up a water buffalo. There was loud laughter and I could make out Bastard, especially. I was tied to the animal and they kicked it to get it going. At first I trotted behind, but then my legs were tied also and I could only take very short steps. I tried to keep up, as one does in sack-racing, and the guards thought this was very funny. Sometimes one of them would come up and push me over. After the animal had dragged me a distance, they would stop him and stand me up, only to knock me over a minute later. I was lucky, though, because the buffalo took it easy and never got it into his head to start running. If he had, I would have broken my neck on the many roots and rocks. The villagers hadn't liked what they were seeing and had all left. I cursed the guards in German, using every word I remembered, and they knew what I was saying. It didn't make any difference, anyway—had I kept silent, they still would have kept right on beating me.

By now it was late in the day. The beating stopped, and again I was given the paper to sign. I still refused. I had no more physical strength but my will to live was still there. I was also angry, so angry that given a chance I would have killed them all, even the province chief, since I figured he had ordered this.

They tried to keep me awake until late in the night, hitting me whenever I closed my eyes. The night dragged on and on as the guards relieved each other. They finally left me alone since they themselves wanted to sleep. I began to cry and cried until I fell asleep. I knew only that tomorrow was another day, that somehow I was still alive, and nothing else seemed to matter.

5 FIRST FLIGHT

The shadows slowly disappeared in the eerie half light of dawn. I wondered if I were really alive. I felt feverish and when I tried to sit up pain shot through my entire body. The guards, usually bedded down two on either side of me, had gone. I was alone and untied, but they knew the pain would keep me from doing much. A guard came in and motioned to me that we were to resume our journey. I didn't see how I could last one hour. Before we left I was given warm rice and more than my usual share of fermented fish. Chewing was so intensely painful that I could eat only a little and the rest of the rice I made into a ball which I stuck into my pocket. My shoes and bag were lying on the ground and it amazed me that they hadn't been taken. I crawled over and put them on slowly even though the guards acted as if they were in a hurry.

I still had my two permanent guards, Bastard and Thief, as well as five new ones. A few villagers and one home guard joined us. Every village had a home guard, a guerrilla with a weapon hidden away, who kept an eye on the villagers.

The guards had to prod me on constantly, since I couldn't manage to keep up. We rested often but never long enough for me to regain any strength. A few hours' march brought us to a village that had been burned but not by bombing, and I wondered if there had been an epidemic here. Twice before we had come across such burned-down villages and each time there was a white line across the trail that the guards wouldn't cross. I later found out that trails so marked led into villages infested with leprosy.

The day was endless and I collapsed numerous times. In the evening when we finally arrived in a village, shouts of *"Bo me kao!"* (no rice) turned us away. A mile beyond, we came to a stand of hardwood trees where there was little undergrowth. Suddenly my guards started to run, shoving me with them. We ran toward several platforms—the remains of old huts—and jumped up on them. Our legs were black with lice—thousands of them. The guards used their towels or parachute cloth, usually worn around their necks, to wipe them off. I forgot about my soreness and concentrated on trying to get rid of the little parasites.

The platform that I was on was about ten feet from the one onto which the guards had climbed. I was shaking lice from my sleeping bag when I saw a machete lying on the ground. The handle had rotted away and the blade was rusty, but it was a weapon. I dropped the bag over the edge of the platform, right on top of the machete, and called to the guards, pointing to it to tell them I was going to retrieve my dropped bag. The lice were back on me as soon as I hit the ground but I was too intent on getting the machete to notice them very much. I picked up the bag and the machete in one motion. I wrapped the bag around my waist as usual, slipping the machete into a loose-hanging fold of cloth to my front, and climbed back onto the platform.

The sounds of a song told us that there was a village nearby, but yelling and banging on our bamboo platforms didn't produce a village guide. Night fell, but still no one came. There was no moon and I couldn't see my hand in front of my face. The guards, growing desperate, shot a few rounds into the air. Finally we saw someone coming toward us, lighting his way by sparking a cigarette lighter now and then. We started to travel in the dark, all bunched up together—one guard had his hands over my shoulders and I in turn had my arms over Bastard's. Like a snake, we slowly followed the villager, who knew every tree and bend in the trail. We began going up at about a 60-degree angle and we all had a difficult time, tripping on roots and slipping on the wet ground. Since everybody was falling constantly,

I wondered if this was my chance to steal the little mirror I had seen in Bastard's tobacco box. He carried the box in his left breast pocket and since my chest was pressed against his back, I would have no trouble reaching that pocket. I began rocking and tripping on purpose, holding onto him and pulling him with me, all the while working his pocket button open. The next time I fell, I quickly pulled out the small box.

I had to work fast, which was hard in the pitch black. Pressing my head against his neck and my arms over his shoulders so he would still feel me there, my hands worked inches in front of him. I threw away the money, knowing the first villager in the morning would pocket it, and then let the tobacco sift through my fingers to the ground. I had assumed the mirror would be loose. Instead, I felt it attached firmly in place by a small frame inside the top of the box. The box was a beautiful, painted thing and I hated to destroy it but I had to have the mirror. I twisted the top of the box back and forth until the hinges broke. I then pulled back the frame to free the mirror, which I stuck into the middle of my rice ball. I figured no matter how well they searched me, that ball of rice would be the last place they would look. I had to get rid of the two halves of the box but I was afraid to throw them away, thinking they might hit a rock and make some sound that would alarm the guards. I cocked my arm and let the broken pieces fly, falling myself with a loud, startled cry to cover the racket. It worked.

To my dismay, we did not walk much farther before we stopped to rest. The voices of the guards sounded excited and I was certain they knew Bastard had lost his box. But when the villager lit his lighter, I could see their unalarmed faces and I relaxed. Then the villager put out a cigarette and lit it. Bastard went for his tobacco and when he realized his precious box, as well as his money, was gone, he jumped up, cursing. He yelled to the villager for his lighter and began searching, flipping his pocket flap as if he had forgotten to button it. When the lighter ran out of fluid Bastard had to rely on the feeble light of the flint.

My heart was pounding as I feared Bastard might retrace our

steps and find the money and pieces of the box on the trail. Probably his belief in ghosts kept him from going back alone along the trail in the dark. He continued his search around the area where we sat but the flint of the lighter was so weak he didn't have a chance of finding anything. We resumed our trek and Bastard cursed all the way to the village.

The village was quiet and seemed to be lacking the usual complement of a dog. I had a feeling that maybe this was going to be my night to escape. Someone carrying a cabang led us across the trail to a porch. It was about five feet off the ground and covered by a lean-to. Thief took away my shoes, as usual, and hung them on the frame of the hut, to my right. The night was lighter now and I sensed the moon had risen. Thief and Bastard worked hastily at tying me down. As they worked I raised my body and arms just enough to give me some slack to play with. They lay down on either side of me and we all went to sleep within minutes; in fact, I was probably the first one asleep.

In his sleep, most likely dreaming, Thief kicked me awake. Both guards were snoring. I made a loud noise but they didn't react. It always amazed me how deeply these people slept.

I was suddenly fully awake, my eyes wide open and every muscle alert. I could see the moon now, not quite overhead. Ever so carefully I slipped my right arm through the loop of rope around it and sat up slowly, looking down at the two snoring guards. None of the villagers was sleeping near us. Getting my ankles out was harder since each was held with a slipknot and the rope was secured five feet under the platform. No matter how hard I tried, I couldn't slip the loop off either foot, and my machete was not at hand. I had to get away! I was already halfway free and would never get another chance like this one.

The bamboo we were lying on was dry and squeaked and crackled at the slightest movement. I lay back slowly and remained still for a few minutes. With all the strength I could muster I kicked both legs upward, holding my feet up to keep them from hitting the bamboo. The slipknots tightened painfully around my ankles but the rope gave way underneath. I let my feet back down and remained motionless. Thief had been disturbed slightly but my fake snoring lulled him back into a deep sleep. I lay there for a few minutes more to make sure he wasn't pretending and even poked him, but he kept on snoring. The tightening of the slipknots had cut off the circulation in my right foot and put it to sleep but I had gained enough rope to work the loop over my foot. After one foot was free, the other came out easily.

I was free—free of my bonds—but the hard part lay ahead. The pain from the beating, my weakness, and the night's cold had vanished, but for a moment I almost decided against trying to escape. Maybe Thief was not really asleep and was waiting for his chance to do me in. I also knew, however, that there would never be a time I could escape without taking a chance. Slowly I inched my way between the two guards toward the edge of the platform. The bamboo crackled with each movement, and my temples were throbbing violently. It seemed an eternity to make the four feet to the edge. Still facing forward, I dangled my legs over the edge of the platform, gripped the bamboo with my hands and let myself down slowly toward the ground. As I let myself down, the bamboo suddenly crackled like a gun going off and the pigs and chickens that were asleep under the hut were awake instantly, squealing and rushing in every direction into the underbrush. The racket was unbelievable. The next thing I knew, I was lying between the guards. How I got there I'll never know, but there I was and my heart thumped heavily. I couldn't believe it, but my keepers were still sound asleep.

I thought about what to do next and decided I had no choice but to take the risk again, right then, as five minutes from then might be too late. I also decided that if I failed again, I would jump up and grab the automatic and shoot it out. Quietly and quickly I made it to the edge of the platform again and let myself down on the ground. Nothing moved and I carefully took my shoes and pulled my bag over the porch, praying it wouldn't snag on the bamboo.

Across the trail, the face of a villager lit up as he took a drag on his pipe. He saw me and I froze. The villager stared at me, got up, turned and went silently into his hut. I wondered if he was getting his gun. I didn't stop to find out and ran along the moonlit trail for a few hundred feet, then stopped to listen. There were no unusual noises. I left the trail; the going was downhill and very steep. Thorns clawed at my feet but I continued barefoot as I wanted to get some distance away before I left any telltale boot tracks. I fell into a mudhole and immediately was covered with leeches. There was no pain, no time to stop—just the cold of the night and the exhilaration of freedom. I passed through a clearing and could see the moon. Then I was in the jungle again, which was totally dark except for an occasional shaft of moonlight slipping through the canopy. Distance was important but it was hard traveling with such a small amount of light. A dog barked and stopped me in my tracks. He barked again but was no closer than before. With the machete in my hand, I felt that I could stop any dog or man who got in my way.

At the bottom of the hill I came across a narrow trail about a foot or so wide. Traveling was easy and fast and even though at times I lost the trail, I would backtrack and always find it again. I came across a little table where there was a piece of bamboo cut like an arrow, pointing in the direction from which I had come. I kept on moving, crossed a downed tree, its trunk whitewashed with moonlight. I had learned enough about the jungle already to know it was relatively safe at night unless I ran into a village.

Minutes were hours and hours were days and I had lost track of time. I was on the trail probably not more than two hours when I again came across a table with a bamboo arrow, and later a white-trunked tree lying across the trail. I'd covered a lot of distance, all right, but in a circle. The village I had escaped from was only a few hundred yards up the hill.

I left the trail and began traveling through the bush toward a tremendous mountain I could see looming up ahead. Moonlight reflected from its bare face. "That's where I'm going, up that mountain," I told myself, and the thought raised my spirits. I thought of climbing it early in the morning when I could use my mirror to signal any passing aircraft. I got entangled in some thorny bush and after I had worked myself free, called it quits. I moved a few rocks, spread out my sleeping bag and zipped myself in to rest for the morning's climb.

At first I couldn't sleep. I thought about what my friends would say tomorrow when the news reached them that I had been rescued. This was going to be my last night in this damned jungle.

I was awake before the light filtered through the jungle canopy. What a pleasure it was to pee without being watched and held by a leash. I didn't waste any time; the guards might already be looking for me. If I reached the mountain before they could find me, I would be safe—they would never think of looking up there.

I passed a musty, foul-smelling pool of water, with the borders marked by millions of wiggling tadpoles and leeches. It hardly looked fit for drinking but I realized there would be no water where I was going. I lay on my belly and drank my fill, cursing myself for leaving my water bottle behind. I picked up pieces of bamboo to make a container but they were all cracked and the water ran out. I decided against cutting down a good container since I figured I had drunk enough to last me until I was rescued.

The mountain was huge all right. If I could make it to the top, I would be completely safe and a rescue chopper could come right in without fear of an ambush. The base of the escarpment was a gentle slope covered with thick elephant grass that stopped abruptly at a cold, gray rock wall rising straight into the sky. I had done a little climbing, and wearing my climbing boots now gave me confidence.

It was not too difficult at first, but then my weakness and pain made me wonder if I had made the right decision. Halfway up would be no good since no pilot would see me from there and no helicopter could pick me up from a sheer wall. Slowly I worked my way upward, blood running from my cut fingers, but I made progress. Halfway up I took a long rest, straddling a tree that had taken root in a fissure in the rock. The view was magnificent. A carpet of greenery as lush as some fairyland spread out below me, with monkeys and white orchids everywhere. Thirst was already getting to me, with the sun just barely over the horizon. I estimated the water hole to be near a large tree covered with dark red leaves. I had to remember this in case I wasn't picked up.

"*Americale! Americale!*" brought me back to reality. The Laotians were calling for me. They were spread out and apparently had been looking for me for quite some time. "Let them look!" I thought. "If they think I'm going to answer, they're crazy!"

Of all mountains I have ever climbed, there was nothing to compare with this one. In a pilots' briefing on the *Ranger*, we were told never to get caught between a karst mountain and the enemy, since such a mountain was impossible to climb. But I had no choice now.

Suddenly I realized I wasn't just climbing a mountain—I was climbing to freedom. The karst leveled off a bit but still rose at about a 70-degree angle. I could look down about 400 feet and my legs started to shake out of control. The mountain was no longer a solid face, but row upon row of sharp ridges. The razor-sharp edge of one ridge was only three or four feet from the next ridge and between them loomed a steep crevasse some fifty feet deep. Sometimes, holding onto vines growing among the karst, I could balance myself and stand atop a ridge. Then I slowly let myself tilt forward, take hold, and swing over the crevasse. Each time, this took great effort and all I could gain was about two feet of altitude.

The guards were yelling and I was climbing. When the ridges got farther apart, I had to climb down into the crevasse to get across. Birds' nests were abundant here but none of them had eggs. I rested more the higher I got, and the view became more beautiful with every step.

I reached a four-foot by ten-foot plateau by late morning but there was no place to sit down since it was covered with thousands of razor-sharp edges. I took off one shoe and used it as a cushion. The little mirror was in perfect condition. I was ready for the planes. "Come on and get me!" I said aloud, smiling. I squinted my eyes against the sky for a glimpse of silver but all I saw was a vast expanse of blue.

I began practicing with the mirror and wished I knew the construction of a signaling mirror—the kind with a center hole. I scraped away some of the silver from the back to have a center hole for sighting. I tried to reflect the sun's rays onto the edges of a nearby ridge, but my aim was off. No aircraft. "Just be patient," I said to myself, "they've come over every morning, why shouldn't they come today?" In fact, the planes from the 0900 launch were probably already on the catapults, if not on their way up north. In the distance I thought I saw Mugia Pass, which I had seen from the air and found hard to forget. This majestic mountain, shaded in browns and purples, formed a quarter circle that began north and curved toward the west.

The sun rose higher and I was getting worried. There was nothing to throw my bag over for some shade and I was sure I would have to climb back down in the evening to get some water if I wasn't picked up that day.

Far below me to the west was a clearing with four well-camouflaged huts. Near them was a field planted with what seemed to be banana trees. I could see acres of trees covered with orchids and other flowers, bright in the intense sunlight. A rise in the ground kept me from looking over the cliff toward the south, but I didn't have the energy to climb the ten feet to take a look. For some reason, I was sure there was a river down there.

The lack of a breeze made it unbearable. I took off my jacket and shirt and threw the bag over my head. I occupied myself with examining my feet and body, which were a mass of bruises and cuts, some festering and some, surprisingly, beginning to heal. Three ticks had burrowed under my right knee. The first two came out easily, but the third was in too deep and I left him there for the doctor on the carrier.

Where the ground fell away to a rocky ledge twenty feet below, there was a small six-foot-high leafless bush. It occurred to me to make a shelter by cutting down branches and then draping my bag over the top to form a roof. On my climb down to it, I noticed a fatty plant growing between the rocks. With the machete, I separated the little growth from its roots. It was fleshy and moisture squirted from the cut. I took a big bite into it to suck out the juices, but no sooner had my teeth sunk into the plant than I felt a tingling sensation in my mouth, almost like an injection of Novocain. I spat it out quickly, unthinkingly dropping my machete into a deep crevasse. It was a quick-acting poison and my mouth had swollen almost completely shut. I tried to wipe my mouth out with my shirt but it was no use and I worried about dying from suffocation. There was no pain, just numbness. My nose was affected slightly but I could still breathe. Then the poisonous action ceased just as quickly as it had begun, and sensation began to return to my cheeks and mouth as the swelling went down.

Now that I had recovered, I tried to reach my machete, but to no avail. It was lost, and with it all hope for a shelter. There was no use in staying there and fretting. If a plane came, it would take me at least ten minutes to climb up to the open, so I went back to my spot.

There was no low-flying aircraft that morning, only the white contrails of jets in the upper atmosphere. After noon, two F-105s came by low, but by the time I saw them and signaled, they had already disappeared into the purple haze to the south. The fact that there was at least some activity raised my spirits and I was certain I would be sighted sooner or later. The sun split my lips and baked my face but I had to remain up on the top. That day the Spads, which flew low enough to spot me, never showed up. There were only a few more jets, one of which dipped his wings in my direction, but then leveled off and headed toward Thailand.

Around 3:00 P.M. I knew that if I didn't get down, I would never make it. Thirst was intense; I was at the point of passing out. I felt sluggish, my head was spinning, and my vision was off. As I started down, I slid and fell, grabbing vines that hung down the face like ropes. My hands bled constantly but I felt no pain, just the sensation of unquenched thirst and the desire to get away from a sun that was killing me. Once I fell down partway into a crevasse and lay looking up at the patch of blue thirty feet above me and about three feet wide, sure I would die there. After resting, I made it out by pulling myself along the vines, straining every muscle in the process.

The jungle top came closer and I kept aiming for those dark red leaves where I hoped the water hole would be. It was easier traveling toward the bottom. In places the vines grew horizontally across the rock, so I could brace myself on them to rest. I didn't care anymore about airplanes, only getting to that water.

Stumbling and falling, I fell into the brownish, scum-filled waters, drinking deeply, paying no notice to the tadpoles. Suddenly a sharp, stabbing pain left me momentarily dazed. Then men were all over me, jerking, yelling, shooting. Fists and feet smashed into my face, and I couldn't open my eyes long enough to see exactly what was happening. A rope was passed around my upper arms and two guards jerked it tight, using my back for leverage. They hauled me to my knees, looped the rope around my neck and then down around my ankles, pulling the rope taut with all the force they could muster. I gagged and yelled. Bastard stood a couple of feet to my left, beating me with a large stick and yelling like some madman.

The news of my recapture brought more guards and all of them had a turn at me. Bastard ripped off my pockets, taking the wad of kip. He threw the rice ball into the bush but, fortunately, he never saw the mirror.

My arms were numb—there was no life in them. Bastard started beating me again while twenty more guards kept jerking on my rope. A guard ran over to me, anger and hatred printed on his tight lips. He tried to hit me over the head with the butt of his rifle, but I moved my head and took the blow on my shoulder. The gun went off as it hit me and a guard nearby yelled and fell backwards. Blood gushed from wounds in both his legs. There was mass confusion and for a minute I just lay there on my side, gagging, thinking I'd probably be dead within a few minutes. Then Bastard was back. He loosened the bonds about my arms, inserted a stick through the ropes, and began to twist the rope tighter and tighter. I yelled out in pain, but the rope around my neck strangled my yell into a gurgle. He kept twisting until my arm seemed to have been torn away. Then he loosened the stick for a second while he inserted another stick under the other arm. Blood rushed into my arm, causing a tingling sensation that made my fingers and hand feel as thick as elephant legs. He tightened the rope again and there was just pain, pain such as I had never known before.

I wondered how I could still be alive. Then somebody tied a rope to my hands and began dragging me down the trail. A little way down the trail I was hung upside down from a tree and beaten until I passed out. Before losing consciousness, I prayed that God would let me die. When I came to I saw blood puddled on the ground directly beneath my head, then tasted the honey one of the guards had smeared on my face. Another came up with an ant nest, a black ball as large as a watermelon. I yelled and shook my head as he broke the ball over my face, spreading thousands of angry black ants all over me. I was semiconscious for what seemed like hours, sometimes realizing what was happening, sometimes not. There was not much pain anymore, only numbness.

I came to, lying on my back on a porch, with soldiers sitting and standing all around me. Some headman stood in front of me. I had to struggle just to sit up. The ropes were gone but my left hand was completely numb and I had no control over it.

The headman, dressed in gray trousers with the cuffs rolled up nearly to his knees, talked to me, but my mind was so fuzzy I wasn't even sure he was speaking Laotian. He talked very quietly. The guards were totally silent. His face was about a foot away from mine and he spoke as if I understood. Occasionally he said something to the guards and they all nodded their heads and then the man continued. Gradually, his voice became louder until it was a shrill yell.

The guards sprang up from the ground, yelling with the headman and pointing their rifles at me, and the headman quickly stepped back. He quieted the guards down and started all over again, raising his voice and working the guards up. I tried to remain sitting because I didn't want to insult this man, but finally fell back from weakness. He had an American .45 automatic strapped to his side and he saw me looking at it and grinned. Taking it out and laying it a few feet away from himself, he motioned for me to run for it. The guards fanned out into a semicircle, opening in the direction he pointed. I shook my head. He repeated his gestured order but I couldn't budge. I knew I would collapse the moment I put my weight on my feet. He stuck his .45 back into his holster and began posturing like a boxer, his fists raised and ready to slug it out. He was crazy if he thought I could fight it out in the shape I was in, especially with the guards all standing there. I tried to put my hands in front of my face but my left hand just dangled, and I wondered if it was dead as the result of the tourniquet being left on so long. I was really afraid, as gangrene in this land of no doctors was surely fatal.

Gangrene or not, I knew I couldn't take another beating and I realized I had to make some kind of peace with the guards. Maybe I could make them think I hadn't escaped but had only gotten lost. I kept repeating the word *pai tai*, which I'd heard the guards use whenever I had to go to the toilet, and I slapped the seat of my pants and pointed to myself. Then I closed my eyes and moved my good hand in front of me like a blind man feeling his way across an unfamiliar room. I was trying to tell them that on the night I turned up missing, I had gone to relieve myself in the jungle and then lost my way back to the little village. After repeating my story in gestures a few times, little lights of understanding lit up their faces. Bastard, though, was unconvinced, and he began talking to the rest of the guards. From the few words I knew, I caught the gist of what he was saying, which was, if I'd only gotten lost, why didn't I answer when they called me?

Finally, I was trussed up and pulled off in the direction of a trail. I was dragged, sliding along the ground as they began to run, seven in front of me, the rest behind. They stopped, blindfolded me, and a man on either side held me up. The blindfold slipped a little and I could see that I was being taken up to a small hill of rock in the middle of some rice paddies. At the rock, they helped me up a bamboo ladder leading to a shelf, fifteen feet from the ground. The blindfold was removed and I was taken down a small incline farther inside the cave where there was a hole about seven feet deep and three feet across. They lowered me down into the hole by the rope and left me.

I didn't care anymore if I lived or died. Even the knee-deep water in the hole didn't bother me at first. The round hole where they had stuck me was man-made. My arms were still tied but I tried to climb the walls of the hole a couple of feet to escape the icy water at the bottom, never able to get very far. Not until then did I realize that I didn't have my shoes or my bag, but it looked as though I wouldn't be needing them. I fell asleep at short intervals, pain keeping me awake most of the time. Every time I moved the guards above slammed home the bolts on their rifles, which wasn't necessary since I didn't have the strength left to climb out.

The night was endless. My body had slipped down in the hole like a sack of potatoes. I wished that I had never left that mountain; dying up there would have been much better. I also thought I should never have tried to come down on the same side, as there must have been water on the opposite side, too. If there was a next time, I wouldn't make the same mistake. I was half mumbling these thoughts aloud, but the guards paid no notice. I kept saying there would be a next time, and tried to sleep.

6 END OF THE LINE

My left hand worried me. It hung limply from my wrist and was as useless as a wet dishrag. Without the hand I couldn't loosen my ropes even slightly. If it didn't get better I could never escape. My feet were numb, probably from standing in the water, and I wondered how they would look when I got up.

As early morning light filtered in, I could make out the faces of new guards. They were dressed in blue uniforms and wore pieces of parachute material wrapped around their necks. One of them had a deep cut on his right foot. They motioned for me to come out but I couldn't make it. This angered them and they started yelling at me. The one with the bad foot cocked his weapon and pointed it down at me. I strained, but couldn't budge. I was jammed in. Other guards came over and soon realized that I couldn't come out. A crude rope was passed under my armpits and the guards heaved, but it didn't move me. More help came and finally I was free from the hellhole.

I tried to stand but my legs collapsed under me. Two soldiers began massaging my legs, forcing the blood through them and straightening and bending them until I was able to stand. I still couldn't stand for long, much less walk, but the guards were eager to go. They pulled me up an incline to the top of a ledge where I could look out over a few small rice paddies.

I couldn't believe my eyes. There, doing their calisthenics, were over two hundred soldiers. All of them were quite young. Two soldiers in dark green uniforms were leading the drill. Directly underneath my ledge were sleeping quarters, and six young women were sweeping them out. This was a training camp and I wondered why it hadn't been spotted from the air since the exercise field was quite large and should have stood out noticeably. Right below the sleeping quarters was a large cave, probably for ammunition and supplies.

I was given some rice and some horrible-tasting fermented fish. Just the smell of it nearly knocked me cold, but it was food and I forced it down. A woman gave me some more rice when I finished the first portion. One of the guards handed me his canteen and I was so unused to kind gestures that I didn't know whether to take it. He continued to urge me to drink, then laughed and shook his head when I handed him back an empty canteen. He left for a few minutes, only to return with a full one and again handed it to me. It was good and cold. Water drops ran down its metal surface and just touching it was refreshing. I drank the second one dry, also, and when he motioned to me to see if I wanted some more, I shook my head.

"*Pai tai, pai tai,*" I said to them, and they wasted no time getting me to the ladder. Because of my bad hand I could only make it down with their help. My legs were better now but they had begun to sting and with each step little shocks flashed through them. I was led to the first outhouse I had seen in this country. It was really nothing more than a couple of sticks made into a bench, but it was a welcome sight. It almost made me feel as if I had made it back to civilization. My bad hand made dropping my pants a difficult task, but the guards were patient and, squatting about fifty feet away, stared at the ground and poked their rifles in the dust.

I was led back to the foot of the cave. Two good-looking men, dressed in dark green uniforms, approached. I was certain they were North Vietnamese regulars. They inspected the way I was tied, which they didn't approve, and retied me more efficiently but less uncomfortably than had the Laotians. I was then led around the karst hill and told to sit down beside a truck. Every surface was flat metal so that any bullet striking it would bounce off without penetrating. The tires were deep-treaded and clogged with red mud.

From the moment the Vietnamese had taken over it felt as if a fresh breeze was blowing. Their military training showed and they carried automatic weapons that looked custom-made. Their teeth were brushed and their hair combed. I knew I couldn't fool around with them and if I tried to escape, I had better make it. To my surprise, my shoes and sleeping bag were brought to me as the traveling group formed. There were four Vietnamese, two dressed in the dark green uniforms and the other two in khaki, as well as three Laotians, including Bastard.

It was a beautiful morning and the sky seemed especially blue. The leaves showed a hint of orange and the whole scene looked like Maine or Vermont in the fall, not at all the way one expects a jungle to look.

Exhaustion made me swerve back and forth like a drunk and we made headway only because the Laotians pushed and shoved me along. My shoes were hanging around my neck and I wanted to put them on, but the Vietnamese shook their heads and said, *"Bo me, bo me."*

The trail now broadened and we came upon a young man sitting on a large, fallen log; a Red Cross medical kit was slung over his shoulder. He watched us go by and then jumped up and said something to the guards. They shook their heads, but he was not to be put off. Finally, the guards moved me back to the log and motioned for me to sit down. For the next half hour the young medic tended to my wounds, swearing at the guards all the while. He washed out the cuts and I was able to get a close look at them. They looked better with all the blood and mud cleaned off but they were still a sickening sight, especially my knees and hands. Once the cuts were clean the medic daubed them with Merthiolate. My greatest concern was my left hand, but the medic could do little for it except rub it with some thick black grease. I wondered how long it would take my hand to rot off. The guards didn't relish all this special treatment and they pulled me away as soon as the medic was finished.

I plodded along again, not interested in the surroundings, my only thought on how soon we would rest. Escape was not on my mind yet. Somewhere around three o'clock that afternoon, we came across some construction equipment. One machine looked like a snowplow and one, to my total surprise, was the shell of a Model-T Ford.

Hanoi stood out in my mind. The fact that the Vietnamese had taken over made me certain I was being taken to Hanoi. At least there I would be with men with whom I had something in common, but I didn't relish the idea of brainwashing and war crimes trials. I was so deep in thought, I hardly noticed we had stopped before a hut standing by itself in a small clearing. The whole party climbed inside and I was motioned toward a corner where I collapsed on a sack. The guards cut up a long, green plant, then mixed the cutting with a handful of red peppers from the sack on which I was lying. I had by now grown somewhat accustomed to their tear-jerking hot peppers and enjoyed the salad.

Voices outside grew louder as an old man entered with three beautiful young girls. No one stood up to greet them; instead they mumbled a weak greeting. The guards ordered the girls to cook some food. They made a fire with bamboo and, setting a steamer over it, squatted down to watch the pot boil, all three chewing betel nuts constantly. I wished they had been barebreasted like the older women, but apparently that was a privilege accorded only to those who were married. The girls didn't even look my way.

The old villager wanted to see my ring. He obviously wanted it and no amount of head-shaking on my part could turn him away. I was too exhausted to argue and took it off to let him look at it. He faced the corner so nobody would see him try it on, then abruptly turned and walked out of the hut.

I was still lying there quietly when something caught my eye. I heard a soft flutter and a pigeon, exactly like the kind in Union Square in San Francisco, landed just above my head on the ledge between the roof and the wall. Tears welled in my eyes. I wished it would fly down to me so I could pet it. The pigeon was busy strutting back and forth, dipping forward as if it wanted to fly down. Finally, it dropped right next to my feet and began pecking at rice kernels scattered over the floor. I wished Bastard had not thrown away my ball of rice, for I would have been only too happy to feed the pigeon and make it stay a little longer. I found some hardened kernels of rice in my pocket corners and placed them on the ground close to my good hand. Just then one of the girls came over to get some peppers and the pigeon flew up, hung almost suspended for a moment, made a small circle to gain altitude, and was gone.

A bowl of rice was thrust at me. The bowl was porcelain, beautifully painted with blue decorations. The villager who had brought the rice was the old man who had taken my ring. He kept pointing at the porcelain dish of rice and then at my finger and I realized he was trading the food for the ring. I licked the bowl clean and spread out my sleeping bag. After saying a prayer, I fell asleep and didn't wake until morning.

Rice again, but this was a different kind of rice—light and fluffy, unlike the heavy and sticky Laotian variety. Although this rice digested easily, a few hours after eating it I was hungry all over again. It didn't seem as nourishing as the dark, sticky rice I had been fed previously. I wondered how my body would survive on it.

The toothless villager sat on the porch collecting his kip from the roll of money Bastard had lifted from me. When I saw my engagement ring on his finger, a flame of anger burned through me. I pointed to it, but the old man shook his head. I thought about bringing it to the attention of the regulars but I wasn't sure what they would do. I longed for the ring since it was about the only remaining link to home, but I kept a prudent silence.

We left the village and about three hundred yards ahead we came across one bomb crater after another. We rushed across the area quickly because of the danger of delayed-fuse bombs. The craters were small, like the ones made by the 250-pound bombs carried by jets, much smaller than the bombs on the Spads. Besides, these bombs were way off target and I was sure no Skyraider pilot could miss by so much. They must have been dropped by "jet pukes," as we called them.

Without warning, we arrived at a river's edge. It was muddy

and wide, with only a few narrows. I expected the party to stop and get organized for the crossing but, instead, everyone kept on walking down the embankment without hesitation. The bank was full of tire tracks leading to the river but there was no bridge in sight and the river was too wide and deep for a vehicle to cross. As I started across I didn't sink and found I was walking on something solid just under the water. No wonder there had been no bridges to bomb and the aerial pictures didn't show bridges—they were all under water! The muddy river was a perfect camouflage against aerial reconnaissance.

We came across a creek and silently, in a crouched position, followed its shores to a large, quiet lagoon, where there were big black fish. The leader took one of his grenades, banged its handle on the ground a couple of times, and heaved it into the pool. For a second I just stood there, not comprehending what was happening. Catching on, I dove on my belly, as the rest of them had done already. I counted to three but there was no explosion and when I had reached ten, there was still no explosion and I chuckled to myself. I was almost embarrassed for this sad display of one of their prized Chinese weapons. Suddenly, there was a tremendous explosion and a shower of water drenched us. After the water had settled, many fish floated up in the pool, their bellies glistening in the sun. One of the Laotians jumped in and began scooping them up.

We smoked the fish over the fire and since there was such an abundance, I was allowed to cook my own. The guards squeezed red ants on fish, which added a bit of zest to the white meat.

The loss of the ring was still bothering me and I gestured to one of the regulars that the villager had taken it. At first he didn't understand what I was trying to say, but suddenly they all understood, nodding their heads. They picked up their gear and we backtracked all the way to the hut in which we had spent the night. The leader stepped up to the villager and without so much as a word of explanation, drew his knife and sliced across the old man's fingers. The suddenness and cruelty of this justice took me by surprise. The soldier grabbed the man's hand, pulled off the ring and stuck it on my finger.

We left immediately while I was still trying to understand what had happened. One thing was sure: if I blundered with them, they would treat me in the same, cold way they had taught the villager the wages of theft.

The trail back was the same except for the fishing. We crossed a narrow, freshly cut road where construction equipment was parked in the heavy bamboo underbrush, and stopped on the other side next to a parked Russian truck. I was told to sit on a small anvil in the middle of the dirt road and the whole gang encircled me. The regulars walked over to the parked truck and knocked on the door with their weapons. A Vietnamese climbed out, rubbing his eyes as if he had just awakened. He headed straight for me and shook my hand as if we were long-lost friends. He was handsome and well-dressed in an American sweater and pressed pants.

He proudly showed me his watch and a ring he had made from a shell fragment. I wondered about all this friendliness. I was on my guard but friendship was welcome any time and I responded readily to his warmth. He left for a moment and returned with rice and gravy in a tin can. While he was gone, I noticed other trucks well camouflaged alongside the muddy road. I'd thought earlier that if I could get near some trucks, I might be able to steal a mirror or even a piece of glass and make a signaling device. But these trucks had absolutely nothing shiny on them—no windshields, no mirrors, not even headlights. After finishing the rice and gravy, I kept the can, thinking I could use it in place of a mirror, but they took it away, pointing to the sky and imitating the firing of machine guns.

We were still sitting in the middle of the road when all the guards jumped up and ran as if on command. Nothing seemed amiss, but by the time we were a few hundred feet away, aircraft had already rolled in. I was one of them now, just a man on the ground under attack. Then the ground erupted and everything around us was shaking. Two of the loudest explosions I'd ever heard set our ears ringing, the shock wave raining bamboo and debris all over us. The guards were yelling to each other as wave after wave of explosions and flying dirt swept over us.

Having somehow lived through the capture, it looked as if I might be killed by my own buddies. The screams of the diving jets were just as nerve-racking as the explosions themselves.

We lay there several minutes after the jets had left. Isolated calls rang out among the Vietnamese. Evidently we had all lived through it. I was afraid they would all take their anger out on me, but no one did anything.

We returned to the little anvil and sat down as if nothing had happened. I wondered what the jets were after because the way the trucks were hidden in little coves cut from the jungle and their roofs covered with branches, not even a low-flying helicopter pilot could see them.

Guards dressed in those same blue uniforms walked down the road and joined us. One of them carried a ten-inch bomb splinter on two pieces of bamboo. He brought it over to me and held the hot piece of bomb a few inches from my face as I cautiously moved away. He followed me with it and then threw the splinter into the middle of the circle of guards. Some of them knelt to smell it. They motioned for me to do the same but I wrinkled my nose and shook my head, bringing laughs from my audience. The Laotian guards pointed at me then to the splinter, then to the air and back to me, but I shook my head, saying, "No, no!" Some guards shifted uncomfortably in their seats and I knew they wanted to get going, as I did. Maybe there were delayed bombs lying around and the quicker we left, the better.

As we left, I hoped we'd walk down the road and wait to be picked up by a truck. Instead, we left the road, passing a few huts loaded with ammunition containers, and followed a path into the dense bamboo jungle. The path was so narrow and low that I had a difficult time getting through. Where they walked, I had to bend down, and where they had to bend down, I had to crawl. Bastard, in front of me again, let the branches snap back into my face. I tried to keep my distance from him, but the guard behind me kept urging me forward.

We approached a village very quietly. After the guards made certain that it was deserted, they began stealing whatever they could find. It was a wealthy village, with an abundance of bananas, lemons, and coconuts, but the guards were much more interested in finding tobacco than food. They untied my hands so I could help.

Before long we were stuffing ourselves. The guards laughed at the way I ate. The lemons were almost all peel and what little lemon there was, was bitter. They burned my cut-up mouth, but I needed the vitamin C. The regulars cautioned me against eating the lemons, rubbing their stomachs and making grimacing faces. The coconuts were delicious as they were still young and the white insides were like jelly.

While we were still sitting on the ground, I had formed a slipknot with the rope over my left arm and hoped that the sight of the rope itself would keep them from checking it very closely. It worked for a while but then the rope started falling off and a soldier walking behind me very politely moved it up and tied it loosely.

I was sure that by now we were out of Laos and well into Vietnam. In fact, I figured we must be close to the ocean. Every time we came to the top of a mountain, I looked east hoping to catch sight of it. I decided that if the ocean was so close, it would be my destination after escaping. As we walked I tried to figure out how many air miles we had covered, but we had changed our heading so often it was an impossible task.

We now left the coolness of the bamboo jungle for a grassy plain, baked yellow by the hot sun. A little boy about six years old had taken over as our guide. He kept up a killing pace. We finally came to a lonely and well-camouflaged hut built on a little hill overlooking a large open area.

Every so often I checked my damaged hand for either signs of life or the setting in of decay, but the hand was the same as it had been the day before. I invented a thousand reasons why I couldn't move my hand and hoped that my future fellow prisoners would know. If my arm didn't get better, I knew I wouldn't be able to fly again. I began to beat my hand against the ground, desperately, as if trying to break loose a stuck connection, but that didn't help, either. The beating caused no pain, which bothered me even more, as it meant that nerves were probably damaged or dead.

We spent the night in this hut, but due to the extreme cold

and wind I slept only an hour or so. Early in the morning a group of villagers arrived carrying a squealing baby pig. One of them poked a bamboo stick into the pig's jugular vein and the blood gushed forth into a pot. The pig shrieked once, then died.

A few days before I had watched a dog being killed for food. The animal was beaten to death very slowly. He whined until his legs gave way beneath him, after which he lay on his side with blood running from his nose. I later learned in prison camp that this was the local way to tenderize the meat. I sat in a daze now, wondering if that would be my end, too.

The guards and villagers mixed some peppers and salt with the blood and guzzled them as if they were a special delicacy. In spite of myself, when the aroma of the cooking reached me, I grew hungry and found delicious the chunks of pig I was given with my rice.

When we were packed again and ready to leave, the leader motioned to me and covered half of one index finger with his other hand, trying to tell me I would be arriving at my destination in half a day. It was a pleasant thought but I didn't believe him. Then Thief came over and took my shoes and demanded my socks, which I had stashed in the bottom of my bag. We had not gone more than a few hundred yards when the leader noticed Thief wearing my boots and socks. Without a word of warning, he picked up a stick and hit Thief over the head, yelling at him to take the shoes off. He yanked them away, tied the strings together and hung them around my neck, pointing to them and then to me to let me know again that nothing would be taken from me.

The sun was gone and the skies were a deep gray. Some of the mountain tops were engulfed in clouds. I thought that surely now we must be nearing the ocean and would be able to see it when the trail reached the top of the mountain. As we neared the top, entering the clouds, I felt as if I were in the middle of a San Francisco fog. Maybe it was all in my mind but the taste of salt air hung heavy in the air. We rested on a crude bench at the top for a couple of minutes and then started down the other side. We broke out of the clouds and, to my disappointment, I saw ridge after ridge of mountains in the distance. I had been so positive we were near the ocean! Without warning the guards suddenly stopped and tied my rope tighter and made sure their rifles were loaded. We began to travel rapidly, double time, jumping from rock to rock along a dry creek bed. As we neared a high bamboo fence, new guards came running toward us. They grabbed me away from my old guards and pushed me ahead with their weapons. They led me along a fifteen-foot-high fence, which was an impenetrable wall of cut bamboo with the ends sharpened into points. Suddenly it dawned on me. The leader had said a half day and it was now about noon. This was the end of the line—the prison camp.

7 PAR KUNG: PRISON CAMP

A guard, who looked as if someone had hit him across the mouth with a sledgehammer, walked me around the other side of the fence. There, two young guards, both of them cross-eyed, stood at a flimsy bamboo door, looking at me down the sights of their M-1s. I was led through the door to the first glimpse of my new home.

I suppose I had drawn my image of what a prison camp should look like from the movies. I expected to see rows of unpainted barracks, all enclosed by a high, barbed wire fence with watchtowers at each corner, and in the open ground between the barracks, prisoners shuffling through their daily exercise. But this place was not at all what I had expected.

The guard with the smashed face pointed his weapon at a small hut and motioned me toward it. As we walked I looked for any sign of life, but the place seemed dead and deserted. The prison itself, named Par Kung, was twenty-one steps by twenty-two steps. There was a little hut to the left of the one to which I was being led and two more huts built at right angles to each other. The opening into my hut was covered with a crude set of wooden bars that posed as a door. A center piece, some three inches in diameter, ran from the ground to the roof and to it were nailed five crosspieces spaced at six-inch intervals. This crude door was buttressed by a long crossbar, suspended from two rattan loops. The guard pulled the crossbar out of the loops and swung the door open on its rattan hinges.

"*Bie, bie,*" he yelled to hurry me up, but I took my time, telling him to keep his pants on. I did my cussing in German with a fake smile, to make sure they didn't understand. The guard pushed me inside, slamming the door and locking it with the crossbar. The inside of the hut looked like a coffin, only bigger. It was about eight feet high by eighteen feet long, nine feet wide, and very dark. The walls were made of hammered bamboo matting attached to a frame of six-inch-thick logs and little light could penetrate. The only thing in the hut besides me was a tangled mass of spider webs. Just outside my hut I could see a table and two benches made from bamboo.

I thought I heard a whisper and sat motionless until I heard it again. I was positive someone was whispering "hello" to me. I moved over to the wall where the whisper seemed to come from and called out, "Hey, anybody over there?"

"Psst, don't shout!" came the whispered reply.

"I'm a navy pilot," I whispered.

"What did you say?" asked the voice.

"I'm a navy pilot off the *Ranger*," I replied. "My name's Dieter."

I heard the whisperer repeat my name and the service I was in to someone else. I squinted through a hole in the rattan and could barely make out half of a face covered with whiskers.

"I'm a helicopter pilot. Air force. Name's Duane," the bearded face said.

"What? You must be kidding!" Suddenly it hit me that he was American and that he was speaking English, the first English I'd heard in over two weeks. I felt like crying at the thought of finally having someone with whom I could talk.

"How long have you guys been here?" I asked.

"Two and a half years for the other guys; nine months for me," Duane said.

"You must be kidding!" I really thought he must be crazy. "They told me I'd be released in ten days!"

"Who said that?" came a quick, almost eager voice.

"Some guy that spoke French, some province chief about eight days back. Say, how many other guys are in there?"

"There are five others in here. They're with Air America—or they were, that is!"

What they said about their time of imprisonment just wasn't right. "Did you say two and a half years?" I asked him.

"Shh, someone's coming!" Duane warned.

Just then the guard with the smashed face, whose nickname was "Nook the Rook," entered the compound, carrying a heavy wooden block. It was about three feet long, four inches wide, and nine inches high, with an oval hole chiseled in its center. Nook opened my door and shoved the block inside ahead of him. "What in hell do you want?" I grumbled at him as he pointed to my feet. He grabbed one of my feet and began pulling it toward the block. I broke free of his grasp, realizing the wooden block looked like the stocks the British used for public punishment. Nook took hold of my leg again but I fought back. "You ain't gonna get me in there, you bastard. What in hell's the matter with you?" I yelled at him in English. He let go and climbed back outside to get his carbine. He came back into the hut and pointed the carbine at me.

"Better put it on," came the warning from Duane, "or they're gonna shoot you in the leg."

"But they want to put me in some kind of footblock!" I said, making no attempt to keep my voice down.

"Just put it on. We all have to. If you don't, he'll shoot you in the leg."

I should never have climbed down from the mountain! I should have taken my chances up there. I pulled the block toward me, showing Nook I was going to comply. He lowered his weapon and in eagerness to get the job done, he twisted and shoved to get my foot through the opening in the block. I cocked my foot so it wouldn't fit too easily, but it finally went through the hole. He yelled at me to give him the other foot, which also took him a few minutes to get in place. He leveled the block, and with a long stick he drove a wedge into place. The wedge ran through a hole in the top of the block, separating my two feet, then ran clear through the bottom. He left, slamming the door and laughing as he walked away.

I didn't say a word—just sat there and stared at my imprisoned feet and felt like crying in despair.

"Don't worry about it—you get used to it," came a voice from the other hut.

Happy as I was to have people to talk to, I wondered just how much I could say to them. What if one of them was an informer? I had to try to find out if everybody over there could be trusted. "Hey, you guys," I said. "It was nice knowing you but I won't be around tomorrow. I'm getting out of here tonight." Now, if there was an informer, I'd be dealing with him soon.

"No, don't! Don't be stupid. You'll never make it," Duane called back. "You'll die of dehydration. There's no water out there." My experience on the karst mountain told me he was right. "We have a plan," he called out in a harsh whisper. "Wait 'til you're over here with us and we'll let you in on it."

"Hey, Duane, is there a doctor or anyone who knows about medicine over there?"

"No, why?"

"A few days back they beat me up pretty bad. My left hand is lame—no feeling in it at all."

Before Duane could answer, the guards were yelling at us to shut up. His bearded face disappeared from the crack in the rattan.

"Psst, hey, psst," I called out, but there was no answer. I shifted my position and tried to make myself more comfortable. After a few minutes, I tried again. "Hey, Duane, are they going to take away my shoes? I got something hidden in them."

"Take it out; you're lucky you've still got the shoes. They're likely to steal them at any time."

I was frantic. I had to get the money out of the shoes. I tried like hell to take the tongues apart, but with only one good hand, it was an impossible task. "You guys got something to cut with? I can't get my shoes apart with only one hand!"

"We'll give you something to cut with later when they let us out," someone whispered.

While I waited, I kept thinking about what Duane had said. The two and a half years bothered me most. I still didn't believe it—it just couldn't be true.

A guard came and opened their hut. I slid over to the door and watched the other guys come out. The first one out was Duane. He climbed out backwards, looking over to me. I waved at him and he nodded back. He wore a green, two-piece fatigue uniform and his last name, Martin, was sewn on over one pocket with the words "Air Force" over the other. Duane's hair was long and his face was covered with a light-colored beard. He was only in his twenties but he walked bent over, as if someone had just hit him in the guts and knocked his wind out. Someone handed him a bamboo container. He slipped on a pair of crude sandals, wooden soles with rattan vamps, then walked down the hill and turned left at a rattan clothesline.

The second man, an Asian, followed. He carried a bamboo container, too, and he also took a pair of sandals from the row outside the hut. His name was Procet and I found out later he was a Thai. Procet wore civilian clothes, shabby but clean. His jacket had been stitched together from small pieces of different-colored cloth. The words "Quo Vadis" ran across the back of the jacket. His face was covered with a thick beard, and his smile revealed rows of bad teeth. "Hey, man!" he called out to me, and waved as he went down the hill to join Duane. He emptied his bamboo container, or "piss tube," on the ground.

Y. C. Tou, a Chinese, climbed out next. He was dressed like Procet but his hair was gray, his face old and covered with deep wrinkles. "Take it easy, man," he called softly as he went down the hill.

The fourth man appeared. He had on green trousers, worn white at the knees. His beard was long and red and his abnormally white hands were covered with freckles. From his coloring it was obvious that he was an American. His name was Gene.

Duane hadn't been lying. These guys really had been here two and a half years. Their clothes were old and worn, to be sure, but there was something more than that. When they looked at me I could see the years written on their faces. There was an animal look behind their slight smiles, and their sunken eyes were haunted and hungry.

Duane and the rest had all emptied their containers, urinated, and now were walking around the compound, saying nothing, as they picked up leaves and occasionally raised their heads to look over at my door.

Another man came out of the hut, an Asian, rather good-looking, with thick black hair and no beard. He was wearing worn blue trousers like the guards.

"I am Phisit," he called over my way, but he had to repeat his name several times before I understood.

"My name's Dieter. I'm German; German-born, actually."

"You are?" he asked, with rather an astonished look, his mouth wide open.

"Naturalized American citizen," I said.

"Oh." He took what seemed to be a urine container from the hut and now emptied it into a porcelain bowl. When Phisit started brushing his teeth, I was surprised to see he actually had a toothbrush and toothpaste.

The last man, the tallest of them, Thani, came from the hut and went down the hill. He didn't even look my way. I could tell he was very young. As I watched Thani leave, Phisit came to my hut and slipped me a toothbrush, a bamboo cup, and a spoon made from a coconut shell.

Y. C., the Chinese, had by now worked his way up to me and while he was picking up leaves from the ground, he asked me about the peace talks.

"Something is going on in Geneva, but I really can't tell you anything definite," I told him.

He just nodded his head and reached through my door to shake my hand.

"I'm Dieter," I told him with a smile, and I felt something between our clenched hands. It was a small piece of green glass.

"Don't lose it. Hide it somewhere," he said, and went back to picking up leaves from the ground. Nook yelled something at us and Y. C. answered him in words and gestures. I couldn't tell what they were talking about.

"*Bie, bie!*" a guard outside yelled. I looked through the door to the entrance of the prison camp. Duane walked down a little trail lined with guards on either side, their weapons aimed at him. He was gone only half a minute when shouts came from where he had disappeared and he came back up the trail, pulling his pants as he walked. "That bastard," he said. Another prisoner started down the trail, which apparently led to the latrine.

Y. C. was puttering around my door. Gene came over and introduced himself. As Gene and I talked, the others came over and introduced themselves also. Both Phisit and Procet spoke good English, but I had a hard time understanding Thani.

I rolled the small piece of glass over in my hand, wondering how I could cut leather with such a miserable tool. I asked Gene about it. He said it was all they had and I should be happy Y. C. had even trusted me with it.

The men had been out for not more than five minutes. Then they were shoved back into their hut, except for Thani. He undressed, put on a pair of green shorts, and hung seven bamboo water containers, each about three inches across and four feet long, from a pole over his shoulders. I heard him walk down behind the hut with the empty containers banging together like chimes. He returned in five minutes, all wet, and walked to my hut. He asked me something in broken English but I didn't understand him.

"Do you want some water?" Duane called out from his hut. But Thani had already left my hut for his own, where a guard was waiting for him with the open door in one hand and a weapon in the other. The door was slammed shut and, as the young guard departed, everything became quiet.

At that moment I wasn't worrying about anything other than getting those two bills out of my shoes. The glass was worn and dull and I had a hell of a time. I finally popped the seam and got the money out.

"Don't lose the glass," a low voice called.

I had been in the footblock for only an hour or so and already the rough wood was cutting my skin, driving me mad. I picked the block up with my feet and slammed it down, cursing the Pathet Lao, their army, and the whole damn war. Neither the profanity nor the pounding did any good.

I pulled up the bamboo matting and hung my boots underneath the hut where they would be out of sight. I hoped the guards had already forgotten about them.

Duane called over and said Gene wanted to know who had won the World Series, but I had to tell him I didn't know; that I liked football, not baseball.

During one of the lulls in our conversation, I began thinking again about how to get the block off my feet. When I was hiding the boots, I noticed many pieces of wood lying underneath on the ground, probably left over from the time the hut was built. From where I was sitting, I couldn't quite reach the wood but the hut was built on a hillside and the ground was closer to the floor at the upper end of the hut. I slid over to that end and was able to get a couple of sticks of wood, one long and the other thin and short. The pin on the footblock was tapered at the bottom so all I had to do was drive it back out. Lying partway on my side so I could turn the block over, I tried to hold the little piece of wood against the pin and hit it with the long piece of wood, but with only one good hand I just couldn't do it. I had escape in mind and that damn hand kept me from doing something as simple as opening a door.

I shoved the long stick into the wall. With my good right hand I held the block so that the pin was against the long stick, and then pressed down on my lever with my bad arm. The pin came free, but I decided to drive it in again partway so I could get it out more easily next time.

"What are you doing?" came from the other side. "Don't make such a racket!"

I ignored them. There was no way I was about to sleep with that block on my feet. I rubbed the pin with spit, which made it go in and out more easily, but it still squeaked loudly. I left the pin sticking about half an inch out of the top, hoping that Nook wouldn't remember how far he had driven it in.

The time finally came when rice was brought for the evening meal. The others were let out and silently took their places around the table in front of my hut. They made the usual rice balls, one for each person. "Hey you, open up here, you bastard, and let me out!" I yelled, but Nook the Rook walked away.

"We'll give you some in a minute," Duane whispered to me.

I slid to the corner of my hut so that I was only a few feet from the table. They couldn't see me but I could see them easily through a crack in the matting.

Nook returned shortly, carrying the hunk of wood he had used to drive the pin into my footblock. He also had two keys swinging on a string around his neck. "*Bie, bie,*" he said, waving his hand toward their hut. They responded slowly, dallying as long as they could. All this while Nook was banging the block against the tree in the yard, keeping time to a melody he was humming, while Procet came by and handed me a large ball of rice. All of them, including Nook, finally disappeared into their hut, and I heard the heavy crack as Nook drove the pins into the blocks. It sounded as if only three of them were put into blocks. I wondered what Nook's keys were for. He then slammed their door and walked over to check on me. Everything became silent after he left and I slipped out of my foot yoke almost noiselessly.

"Good night," I whispered to the others. Then I fell soundly asleep.

I was awakened by the sound of the stockade fence being opened. "The block!" flashed through my mind. In panic, I jammed my feet into the holes and slammed the pin home just as my door was opened by a fat guard who was nicknamed "Jumbo."

During the night I had slid down the sloping floor to the opposite corner of the hut. Jumbo waited for me to slide up to him and then without saying anything, he drove the pin out of my block, then left for the other hut. After opening their door he sat in the doorway, picking at large pieces of dead skin on his feet. Jumbo had left my door open but I didn't know if he'd done it on purpose. I had to go to the hole so I climbed out and joined the others in the yard. I expected Jumbo to yell at me but he was silent. Gene told me that Jumbo didn't care one way or the other.

Gene asked a lot of questions that morning. He wanted to know if President Kennedy really had been assassinated. "Hey," he asked, "have they come out with stainless steel razor blades yet?"

I didn't know, but I was sure they had. I told him that no one could even buy the old ones anymore.

"You're kidding," he said. "Are you sure about that?"

"Of course, I'm sure."

"Well, I'll be," he mumbled to himself. "That's what I wanted to invent when I got out of this hellhole."

That made me feel bad because I didn't know for sure and I hated to take away his hope. But before I could say any more, Gene began talking about beer and then about other things. He sounded a little kooky to me.

Y. C. came past us as we circled in the center of the yard, asking for his piece of glass back.

Phisit inspected my hand with the care of an examining doctor, but the cause of the lameness was a mystery to him. He suggested that I massage it with hot water.

"Where would I get some hot water around here?" I asked.

"At breakfast time they're going to bring warm bark water. You could use some of that."

Jumbo ordered us back into our huts. I walked with Phisit, hoping Jumbo would let me in with them. Phisit even tried to convince him, but Jumbo insisted I go back to my own hut.

"Pretty soon you're going to be with us," Duane said. "Just don't worry. Take it as it comes."

Around midmorning the "punk" of the camp, whom the others had affectionately dubbed "Little Hitler," came in and talked with Phisit and Procet. Then I was told that I was to be interrogated in an hour or so. Procet was to come along to translate. I about dropped dead.

That formal word, "interrogation," brought to mind all sorts of images of torture and brainwashing. Even the guards treated this as some sort of an official affair. They all had on their best uniforms and had loaded their rifles conspicuously. Little Hitler led the parade, glancing back now and then to be sure the others were still with him. My heart started to beat fast—I was scared; and Procet didn't like it, either. I was sure I'd be beaten again. Little Hitler came toward me, followed by Kid, Nook, and Windy. Windy got his name because he sang propaganda songs by the hour. He was the nice-guy type who would laugh with you one moment, then squeal to Little Hitler the next.

Outside the prison entrance we were joined by Jumbo. The remaining guards waited for us near their huts above the camp. The Vietnamese regulars were sitting on a pile of logs. I thought they had left the day before but they had apparently spent the night at the village nearby, probably because of the girls there.

Procet said he didn't like the setup at all—there was something weird about it. All four Vietnamese were there—one of them with a little pad of paper in his hand.

"What's your name?" he began. He carefully recorded every question and every answer on the paper.

"What kind of aircraft did you fly?" he asked.

I wasn't supposed to tell that kind of information to the enemy but after I talked it over with Procet, both of us decided it would be better to tell them something instead of nothing. I told him to stick with my photobird story. Procet began talking his head off and I became uneasy. When the tension became too much for me, I asked him what he was telling them, and not to say anything about the Spad.

Procet stared at me silently in a way that made me wonder whether I should have interrupted him at all. He resumed talking to the leader and after a while asked me how many engines my aircraft had.

"Tell them if they will untie my arms, I will draw them a picture."

After being untied, I used a twig to scrape an airplane on the ground with nine engines on the wings, four on the right and five on the left. Procet felt I should put another engine on the right wing to keep things balanced but the leader was copying the drawing on his pad and I thought I'd better not make any changes. Then they wanted to know how many men were in my crew and who they were. All along I'd been assuming they had found my plane, but this made me wonder. My plane obviously held only one man and if they'd found it, they would have known I had been alone.

"Tell them the truth," Procet insisted. "Maybe they didn't believe your nine-engine aircraft."

"I was alone," I told the Vietnamese through Procet. "I was the only pilot and there were no crew members."

One of them didn't take that for an answer, so Procet once more began talking nonstop. The longer Procet talked, the more I was sure he was giving out all the information that I had told him in the morning. I interrupted him, which made him angry, and he told me that if I didn't like what he was saying, I could tell them myself.

The Vietnamese seemed to take everything at face value. Little Hitler and his gang seemed anxiously waiting for the word to work us over, but it never came. When the regulars gave orders for us to be returned to our huts, Little Hitler seemed to think we'd been let off too easy. As soon as we had gone around the corner, he kicked me in the back. I yelled loudly, hoping that the regulars would hear it and come over, but they didn't. Back at my hut, the guards locked me into my block and left.

"That wasn't too bad," Duane said from the other hut, "and I'd sure like to know what kind of aircraft has nine engines."

Later the others were let out to eat. After breakfast Gene brought me his blanket and told me I could use it. I didn't want it since I was sure it was the only one he had, but he kept insisting, saying that Duane's was big enough to keep the two of them warm.

The morning was boring and slow-moving. I started making

my escape plans again. "Did you guys try saving rice?" I asked.

"Yes, but it's no use. It just rots and turns green."

"Did you try to dry it?"

"How're you gonna dry it?"

"Lay it out on the floor or on some material," I answered impatiently.

"Oh, yeah? And what're you gonna do if there's a surprise inspection?"

They were right. If a guard walked in and found a supply of rice laid out to dry on the floor of my hut, it would be tough to explain.

The idea of rotting away for years, plus the boredom of waiting, worked on my mind. I needed to prepare for my escape. Now.

Thani had the best ear and spoke Laotian well. His job was to sit with his ear glued to the wall and eavesdrop on the guards. In the afternoon, Thani told us the Vietnamese had packed up and would be leaving shortly. Everybody breathed a sigh of relief. I was glad because it meant I wouldn't be subjected to a second interrogation, but then I began to worry. With the Vietnamese gone, the Laotians might help themselves to my few belongings. Gene told me they had lost everything, and he couldn't believe I still had some of my stuff left.

The nylon bag was particularly valuable. All our clothes were badly ripped and the bag could furnish us with thread. Y.C. offered to lend me a needle if I gave him some thread. I began ripping up the bag. I had in mind to make myself a type of flight suit and a rucksack for the big day.

I saw Nook start to come my way and I quickly stuffed the torn bag under me. He opened the door and from his hand gestures I realized he wanted my shoes. "Not on your life, mister!" I said to him, but then acted as if I didn't understand what he was saying. Nook yelled over to Procet to translate, but even after Procet put it into English, I shook my head. Finally, Nook began looking for the shoes himself and found them dangling under the floor. Without even looking at me, he left with them.

At least the money was out of them but even so, the shoes were a great loss to me. Thani called over to say he'd seen Nook hang my boots with theirs.

I was still thinking about my shoes when Jumbo came in and knocked the pin out of my block and let me out to eat with the others. It was crowded at the table with an extra person, so Gene volunteered to sit on the crossbar that connected the benches on each side.

"There's a good chance of your getting over with us tonight," Phisit said.

"I sure hope so. The mosquitoes are driving me crazy over there." I found out that the others had been issued mosquito nets.

I was pleasantly surprised when the guards brought us hot bark water. I decided not to save any of it for my arm since there were too many thirsty men here. Thani, in particular, had a real water problem. He was thirsty all the time. During the night he could polish off a whole water container all by himself. The bark water did us a lot more good than the regular drinking water, which turned stinking in a day.

Gene began telling me about the old days, before Little Hitler took over the camp. "When the Old Man was in charge, we were allowed to make little fires inside the huts and boil our own water," he said. "But now that this bastard, Little Hitler, is here, we can't have anything." Gene pointed out a few plants growing near what seemed to be the kitchen hut. "Those are our famous mustard plants," he told me. "The Old Man let us grow them, but not anymore."

"The damn guards just trample them to get us mad," interjected Y.C.

"Look over by the gate," Duane pointed toward a few tiny plants with small, red, and nearly leafless stems. "Those are tapioca plants. We planted those, too, but now the guards piss on them for fun!" Y.C. grew more and more angry and the veins on his thin head swelled into little ridges.

The guards let us out to use the latrine. I told myself I would take my time since I wanted to look around for a possible escape route, but I'd barely gotten my pants down when the guard we called "the Kid" started yelling, *"Bie, bie,"* at me. I pointed out to him that I hadn't even gone yet, but he just got furious and pointed his carbine at me. I hurried back to the camp with my pants still halfway down, swearing I'd get even with him. The others just laughed at me. Suddenly my swearing and their laughing were silenced by a shot and a cry coming from the direction of the hole. Duane was down there. Gene anxiously called out, "Are you all right, Duane?"

"I'm alive, if that's what you want to know!" Duane yelled back as he hurried up the trail to the compound. His face was snow-white and his neck was bloody. Ten guards followed him in, and before we could find out what had happened, they herded all of us into the hut. The guards slammed the door and fled.

"What in hell happened?" we asked Duane.

"Well, hell, I just got my pants down when Nook yelled at me to get back. He didn't even give me a chance to open my mouth or pull up my pants before he fired at me." The bullet had scraped his head above his right ear—another quarter of an inch and he would have been dead. None of us said anything but we were all thinking the same thing—any minute could be our last. I knew I had to get away.

My new home was a small place, about eight by fifteen feet. A couple of clotheslines ran the width of the hut. Some yellow mosquito nets hung on the wall. Pillows made of leaves designated the individual sleeping places on the floor. Some chopsticks, a couple of blankets, a few bamboo containers, and a small fan fashioned from long feathers were piled in one corner. A piece of split bamboo hung overhead with three labels stuck to it—Oscar Mayer, Campbell's Pork and Beans, and a fragment with the word Silicon. The last thing I expected to see in a Laotian prison camp was a collection of American tin can labels.

"Whose is this?" I wanted to know.

"That's Gene's, and don't touch it!" Duane said.

"How did you get them?" Just the sight of them made my mouth water.

"About two years ago," Gene said, "I got a small package

from home. It'd been much bigger but the PLs had taken most of it and all that was left were six capsules of some kind of medicine and three cans of food, two of them empty. But they all still had their labels on so I took them and hung them up there." Gene was obviously proud of them.

My fellow prisoners gave me an official welcome that evening. We raised our bamboo cups of bark water and made a toast to a successful escape.

Duane's bullet wound wasn't deep and the bleeding had just about stopped. Nook came in about an hour later to put us in blocks and I was handcuffed to Procet since he was the only one who had a mosquito net just for himself.

Then Duane began to tell me their favorite prisoners-versus-guards tale. A couple of weeks before I was brought in, the guards refused to let the men out to the latrine, so they had to use their containers. When they got full, the men still weren't allowed to go out, so they heaved the cans out into the compound yard. Pretty soon it began to stink like hell and the guards began wearing towels over their noses and mouths. But they still wouldn't let the men out. This went on for more than a week. Little Hitler came in one day to give them hell about the mess they were making. Gene was so mad, he threw his container out in the compound, aiming for the ground in front of Little Hitler. The container flipped as he threw it and the whole mess landed on Little Hitler's feet. He screamed in anger and fear. To a Laotian, the body below the waist is taboo and he was sure he had been defiled. He came down hard on them and all their privileges were taken away and their food cut off for three days.

Gene slid over to the door and covered it with a makeshift windbreaker so that the guards couldn't see us, and we all took our footblocks off. What really surprised me, though, was that they were able to get out of the handcuffs. They had first made a workable key from a quill but it was so flimsy it could be used only a couple of times before breaking. They tried unsuccessfully to make a wooden key. Finally, they scrounged all the toothpaste containers they could find and melted them in Y.C.'s can. It was a lengthy job which consumed an enormous amount of charcoal and took even more blowing. They had made a die for the key—a thin stick of wood wrapped with thread to simulate the threads of a screw which then fit into a piece of wood with a hole in it. The lead was poured into the hole and allowed to cool. It took them several tries before they finally got a key that worked.

Getting the cuffs off was still somewhat of a job. They were big, old French ones with two wrist rings connected by solid metal bars, which meant that if one of us moved, the other man had to move with him. Procet kept his key rolled in a strip of rag hidden in his shorts. After he took the key out and screwed it into the keyhole, I put pressure on the two connecting bars and Procet gave them a good pull, whereupon the cuffs opened. It was really important to keep the pressure on them because if we let go too quickly, the spring made a hell of a racket coming apart.

We helped each other out of the footblocks and crawled under the mosquito net. We laid the cuffs and our blocks nearby so they would be handy in case there was a surprise visit. When Nook was putting us into the cuffs and blocks, he also tied a rope around my arm and passed it outside through the wall so that any passing night guard could give the rope a jerk and make sure I was on the other end. I took the rope off and tied it to a support pole in the hut. Then Procet and I lay back and listened to Duane tell the story of the Greeks and the Trojan horse.

Night guards were stationed in the other hut across from us, where they squatted and smoked their little bamboo pipes. One guard looked like a true madman. His hair stuck out as if he had been permanently frightened, his eyes were badly crossed, and his movements were strange and spasmodic. The others had nicknamed him "Moron." Since there were no clocks, the crowing of the chickens in the morning signaled the time when the guards went off night duty. Sometimes, in the middle of the night, Moron would crow like a chicken so he could get off duty and would then look for a warmer place to spend the rest of the night.

"Hey, you guys, I have to go!" Little Y.C.'s voice broke my sleep, interrupting a beautiful dream. Y.C. was almost always the first one up as he usually had to go pretty badly. No one wanted to hear him because we had to get into our cuffs and blocks before calling the guards to let him out.

"You guys better hurry up, or I'm going to smell this place up again!" Y.C. warned.

"You do and I'll kick your ass," Procet whispered.

"Pai tai, pai tai!" Y.C. yelled as loudly as he could.

Finally, Jumbo lumbered in and unlocked the door. Y.C. ran down to the gate and stood there shouting, *"Pai tai,"* and waiting for someone to come.

We brushed our teeth with Chinese toothpaste, which tasted like peppermint and, in fact, the tube was marked with a Wrigley's spear. I ate my share of the toothpaste instead of wasting it on brushing my teeth.

We walked around the yard in a circle, keeping our eyes to the ground to avoid looking at each other. These moments of privacy were very precious to us. The air was full of the smell of singed hair, which meant the guards had trapped an animal. My mouth began to water and Thani went over to the fence to talk to the guards and see if we were going to get some meat. He came back with downcast eyes and told us that the guards had caught a couple of rats but that they had eaten them while cooking our rice. The rest of the guys were really unhappy but somehow I was relieved. I hadn't yet learned to like rats, but my time would come.

I went into my former hut and nonchalantly gathered up my blanket, bag, utensils, and money and quickly shoved them into my new home. I was wondering where to hide my money, and Duane suggested I hide it in my skivvies, that being a taboo area. He showed me what he had hidden there—a little knife made from an ammunition clip, his wedding ring, and a piece of mirror about the size of a quarter. Gene thought a toothpaste tube would do and I liked that idea better. We opened up a nearly empty tube, licked it clean, then folded the two bills neatly and stuck them in the tube. When I had finished putting it together, the tube bore no traces of tampering.

"Put it in your skivvies," Duane kept saying, but I thought

it was less conspicuous on the wall with the rest of the toothpaste tubes. I could feel Duane's resentment because I didn't follow his advice, but I figured it was my money and I could do with it what I thought best.

After breakfast we were put back into the hut. Nook came inside and began putting me in my block. I refused to cooperate since the other guys were not being locked in. This made Nook mad, and after he had forced my ankles into the block and set the pin, he locked the handcuffs on me, as well. Then he tied a rope to my right arm—the good one—and passed it out through a slot in the wall. He pulled on the rope until my arm was held high over my head, then tied the rope fast. I could see this was going to be a rough day. I couldn't take a chance on getting out of the cuffs and block during the day, as the guards dropped in unexpectedly.

Duane and I weren't talking and I thought, "He's so damn slow. Anyway, he's an air force chopper pilot."

Procet had produced a knife from somewhere and was carving an aircraft, a C-47, on a cup. Duane had a helicopter on his bamboo cup. That meant I'd need a Spad on mine.

"I'll give them my left arm tomorrow," I announced, "but I'll take my jacket off first."

"Better yet, why don't you graciously accept the blocks next time?" Y.C. needled me in a joking way, and they all laughed.

Many days passed like this. Sometimes we quarreled. Actually, with the cramped quarters, the bad food, and the boredom, it was a wonder we didn't start killing each other. But we also laughed a lot. There was nothing funny about our situation, but sometimes the laughter hit us so hard that I thought my stomach would burst.

One evening we were sitting around the table eating our rice, when Thani looked up and nudged Phisit, who was sitting next to him. We all looked up and saw Little Hitler come into the compound. He walked around, looking at the mustard plants that the guys had planted when the Old Man had been in charge. He was up to something. Procet and Phisit got up from the table and walked over to him. Little Hitler began talking to them. From their expressions, we knew it was good news.

"Something about a release," Gene whispered. We all stopped eating and strained to hear. Gene had learned enough Laotian to get the gist of what they were talking about at first. But now Procet and Phisit were talking so fast to Little Hitler that Gene couldn't keep up.

"What'd they say? Come on, man, tell us," we urgently asked the two Thais when they returned to the table.

They smiled at each other with big smiles and said, "They want us to eat the mustard plants and then pack up. We're going to be released!"

"You're kidding? This is it!" I yelled out. "To hell with this rice. Come on, tell us what all he said! Did he say anything about the Geneva Convention, or is the war over?"

"Little Hitler just told us that we were to eat the plants tonight and then pack, since we'll be leaving for Yamalat in the morning."

"Yamalat!" Duane said with a smile across his face.

"What's in Yamalat?" I wanted to know.

"Hell, that's where the province chief is," Gene answered.

If they held us there, we stood a better chance of escaping to Thailand. Duane also told me that Yamalat was their headquarters and that meant adequate food and medical supplies.

I looked around the table and saw the troubled looks on the guys' faces. Nobody seemed happy except for me. "What's the matter? Think you're going to be homesick for this place?" I jokingly said to them.

"First of all," Gene began, "all the Pathet Laos are lying bastards and nothing they told us before ever came true, especially when it came from that little no-good son of a bitch."

True or not, everybody began to brighten up. We discussed what we should take along with us. Thani had stolen a machete that he kept buried under the tapioca plant. We wondered if it wouldn't be better to leave it behind. If it were true that we were going to be released, we wouldn't need it and if it were found during a search, it might do us more harm than good. We decided to leave the machete.

That night we were given some cooked bamboo shoots with the rice and even though they weren't nutritious and only gave us the "trots," they were a sign of better times. We were also allowed more time at the hole and, when we were returned to our hut, the guards didn't put us in the blocks.

I didn't have much to pack—a cup, toothbrush, a pair of chopsticks, the remains of my nylon bag. I hid my money in my jockey shorts.

I was surprised when we were put in handcuffs and blocks that night. But I figured that the guards certainly didn't want to suffer the disgrace of losing one of us on the last night. "What the heck, we can hack one more night of this," I said. We all sat around, talking about being free.

Windy had been singing his propaganda songs for a couple of hours and was still going strong. He sounded like a priest chanting the Mass in Latin, all in a monotone. As I lay there listening, I remembered that the province chief had told me I would be released in ten days. The idea startled me. "Hey, you guys, I told you the province chief told me I would be released in ten days. So this must be it!"

"Be quiet, damn it, I wanna sleep," Y.C. complained from his end of the hut.

"Sleep?" I said. "A time like this and you want to sleep? You must be nuts!"

"Knock it off, Dieter," Gene told me in a low voice in my ear. "Don't argue with Y.C. Someday I'll tell you something you don't know."

I rolled over and and slept soundly until morning.

After breakfast rice we waited outside for the final preparations to leave. I began to feel dizzy. Just standing up was a big job. Of all mornings, I had to get a fever now. Gene asked if he could help, but there was nothing he could do except tell me to hang on. When they were ready, Little Hitler and Nook came in and inspected our hut. The rest of the guards arrived and put us in handcuffs. They slipped a rope through the loops of the cuffs. A guard to the front and one to the back held onto the ends of the rope.

"What's the rope for?" I asked Duane. "I sure don't plan to run away." Duane didn't answer.

Procet was up front followed by Y.C., Phisit, Thani, Duane, me, and Gene. Five guards were in front of Procet and the rest were behind us. They took us through the village where the villagers sat on their porches, chewing betel nuts and spitting out the blood-red juice. We crossed the creek and climbed over some large rocks and continued along the trail I'd been brought down a few days earlier.

Sick with fever, I dragged behind, making it difficult for the others to walk. Gene kept pushing me on to save himself and me from a guard with badly bucked teeth who had earned the nickname "Crazy Horse." I moved just as fast as I could. I knew the trail climbed straight up for a while and that there was a bamboo bench at the crest of the trail. I put one foot after another and just kept moving. What I didn't understand was why, this close to freedom, Crazy Horse had to harass me.

I remembered the trail very well and knew that there was a junction only a few hundred yards downhill from the crest. There the trail split—one going to the left, the other to Yamalat. We took the trail to the left, and the last thread of hope was cut. I cursed myself for leaving my spoon and Thani's machete behind. We knew for sure now that we were being moved to a new camp.

The trail led us through rice paddies and into dry creek beds with large maxan trees, their sour fruits strewn around them. Maxan tasted terrible and was very fibrous but it was a good source of vitamin C. I picked up three and began chewing on them as we walked. My step count was up to 6,336 from the junction when we arrived at a fence. We prisoners looked at each other and, without saying a word, knew this was our new home.

8 HOI HET: NEW HOME

"Those lying bastards," I thought as we neared the fence, "wearing a guy down by promising something, keeping him around until he's a vegetable with neither strength nor will to break out. Not this guy! It won't work with this guy! Just wait, I'll get out of here!"

The name of our new "home" was Hoi Het. This camp was built very much like the other one except that it was much better camouflaged. We stashed our belongings inside our appointed hut and decided who was going to sleep where. With everything in place, we all climbed out and walked about the yard.

"*Bie, bie!*" yelled Little Hitler, quickly walking up to us. We turned around toward the hut, but he kept on yelling. He began arguing back and forth with Phisit and Thani. It gradually became clear what he wanted—to split us into two groups. Phisit, Thani, Y.C. in one side of the divided hut, the rest of us in the other.

Nothing had really changed—the same old routine lay ahead —except that now our plans to escape became serious.

The first thing we had to do was choose a good date for the escape. Many things had to be considered in this choice. We had already decided we would try to find a river and float out, traveling by night and hiding by day. That meant we needed an early moon for light to guide our way to the river and then pitch darkness to cover our getaway downstream. The others told me about the torrential monsoons that kept the guards huddled in their huts. The heavy rain would also cover any noise, and it would wash away our tracks in a matter of minutes. In addition, I liked the timing of the rainy season. The year before, the rains had begun on May 15 and lasted for a solid month. If they came on schedule again this year, I'd be a free man on my birthday, May 22.

On the third day after we arrived at Hoi Het, the guards took us to the nearby creek for a bath. The water was cool and invigorating, a real treat, but we made it part of our escape plan as well. The trail leading to the creek twisted its way through the jungle for three hundred yards. We all counted paces from the main gate to the creek and tried to remember the paces from one important checkmark to another. Back at the hut we laid out little sticks to represent each mark to scale. Soon everybody knew the trail by heart.

Though we had picked a date and a time, we still had to decide on a method of breaking out. This became a subject of no little debate. My idea was to steal weapons from the guards, kill them, and take all the food in the camp; but none of the others liked the idea. According to the Geneva Convention a prisoner of war who had killed or harmed a guard while escaping could be executed on recapture. None of them wanted to take that chance. In fact, Phisit wouldn't take part in any plan at all. He told us he wouldn't save any rice and did not intend to join us. He thought the whole idea was crazy—he wasn't going to get himself killed because of some escape-happy guy like me. His reluctance made our planning very difficult, as we had to make sure we escaped in such a way that the Pathet Lao didn't take revenge on him.

We decided to make a couple of changes in our routine, changes that might give us extra time when the escape day came. We convinced Y.C. to stop his early morning visits to the crapper. The guards hated having to let him out and they wouldn't make any effort to come over for Y.C. if he didn't make all that racket. Y.C. stopped yelling and used a container instead of going to the hole. The first day the guards still came over from force of habit, but after that they stopped coming until it was time for the morning rice. Although we all missed the ten minutes of exercise that Y.C.'s toilet calls had meant, this change in routine added an extra two hours to the time we could travel before the guards would know we were gone.

Part of the trouble with developing a good, solid set of plans was the petty fighting among us. At first Duane and I were in constant conflict about the escape method. However, as time passed we became good friends. His religious hard-headedness mellowed to the point where he promised to get drunk with us once we got out. Then Procet and Y.C. became quarrelsome. We'd decide something, and one or the other would change his mind and get mad, refusing to talk to anyone. The silent treatment was a standard prison camp gambit. Gene told me that Phisit and Y.C. had had an argument once and hadn't said a word to each other for over a year before they finally made up. I found that hard to believe, but the more I got to know them, the more I knew it could have been true.

All of us except Phisit participated in saving rice and our store grew larger. We dried it for three days, moving it to a different rag each day to keep count. We then put it into the four sacks Gene had sewn from scraps of my nylon bag. We let the rice dry in the sacks for two more days and then we hid the sacks in the extra waste container.

It took us a while to figure out how to store the dried rice but finally we hit upon a good solution. We'd cut down one of the long bamboo poles that held up the leaf-covered frame of the roof. Singing to cover the noise, we used a long hardwood stick to break out the thin walls separating the various compartments in the bamboo stalk, thus making it into a long, continuous tube. We then filled it with rice, plugged the open end, and put it back in place in the roof. Only the rats knew where our stash was hidden. We could hear them at night, chewing on the bamboo, hoping to get to the rice. Twice we found the plug gone but most of the rice was safe since the tube was too narrow for the rats to enter. After we'd collected what seemed to be enough rice, we called a halt to the operation.

Now we had to wait for the rains. It turned out to be a long wait. The water situation kept getting worse. After our first bath, we were allowed to bathe every two weeks, and after a while, not at all. A little puddle of water, just large enough to hold one person, was all that remained of the creek. The little pool of stinking water filled with wriggling larvae was our drinking water, but the guards also used it to wash themselves and to clean the game they shot infrequently. The water stank, and when it was poured into a cup we couldn't see the bottom because of all the algae and worms. But thirst has a way of putting an end to queasiness. We drank it anyway.

Nook was the great hunter among the guards and whenever he came in and wanted our urine containers, we were excited because it meant he was going hunting. He took the containers into the jungle and emptied them on some cut bamboo he'd scattered on the ground. Hoping the deer would come to lick it, Nook lay in wait for them. We in turn would lay in wait for Nook's gunshot. At the first shot we held our breath and prayed there would be only one shot, as two shots would mean he had missed. One shot meant there was a good chance he would bring something back. If he did bag an animal, word traveled fast and the villagers would arrive at the camp even before the game was carried in. Since this was their valley, they had a right to a share of the meat. By the time the villagers and the guards took their share, only the intestines remained. The gut was sliced open, its contents dumped on a large banana leaf and given to us. We were so desperate for food that we didn't even bat an eye as we wolfed it down.

The other men told me that the past year had been bad, but this one was really the lowest point. The two previous years they had had all the rice they could eat. Now it was only one meal a day, and we knew it would be reduced to less in time. We wondered if it wouldn't be wise to go into our stash of rice but decided against it, as that would have meant forfeiting our chance of escape.

The guards were also getting smaller and smaller rations. The less food they had, the meaner they became. They had taken to firing at us when we went down to the hole. They wanted us to die because every bite we ate meant that much less for them. We were aware they had murder on their minds, so we began to crap only in the containers, using our evening run to the hole for emptying the containers in order to reduce our exposure.

But the privilege of the evening run to the crapper was, like all our privileges, gradually eliminated. Soon it was no water, no toilet, and no going outside. But the worst thing was that we were kept in newly made large blocks. We had to sit in one place all day, cuffed to each other, sweltering in the mosquito-ridden heat and gagging from the fumes of our shit.

Procet heard one night that the famous Old Man was returning soon from his two months' trip to find rice for the camp. Everyone was overjoyed, thinking of better times to come. We eagerly waited for the Old Man the next day and the day after and the day after that, wondering if he would bring some mail, some good news, anything. After the fourth day of waiting, our hope was almost gone. Gene was sitting by the door looking out, when all of a sudden he straightened up. There was some commotion outside and Duane and I slid over next to Gene. "It's the Old Man!" we all said, and our hearts pounded with expectation. First he visited with Y.C., Phisit, Procet, and Thani, then walked around to our side of the hut.

The Old Man opened our door. His high forehead was furrowed in a scowl and his lips were pursed, wrinkling his dark, leathery skin. His face was kind and we waited for some good word. We asked about the war, the Geneva talks, and the mail. As we poured out the questions, he only shook his head, casting his eyes down and away from ours. There was no news, no mail, nothing—not even the blanket and mosquito net Duane had been promised. After a few minutes he turned away and left. We three just sat there staring out of the crack of the door, as if we were still waiting for the Old Man, the one who was coming with the good news.

In the weeks that followed, the food was more scarce and the guards took turns going on rice missions. It took them three to four weeks to make each trip, and on the return journey the guards and village porters would eat over two hundred pounds of rice. By the time they returned to camp, there was hardly enough grain to last a week. The guards weren't smart enough to ration rice and when the supply ran out and the rice party had not yet returned, the guards ran around yelling, *"Ba, ba,"* and sang about how hungry they were. Their wailing made us nervous.

One day we were all lying on the floor, discussing our escape plans, when Duane looked at the ceiling. "Listen. Do you hear it?" Duane asked, his eyes still roving over the ceiling and down the walls of the hut. I was about to answer when I was drowned out by the noise of the heavy pounding of the first rain. It was not the monsoon season yet and this rain was comparatively mild and would stop in time. But it was a sign of what was to come.

"Hey, Duane," I yelled at the top of my lungs, but he could barely hear me.

"Wow, listen to it. Wait until the monsoon season hits—it's even louder then," shouted Gene. We were whooping and hollering, hitting each other, happy with the thought that our plan would work after all.

"Come on, baby, pour, will ya!" Gene grinned from ear to ear as the rain answered his bidding.

The roof in our half of the hut started leaking. Procet, Gene, Duane, and I complained about it until they let us move to the hut across the way. Y.C., Phisit, and Thani were left where they were. Procet talked to the Old Man and was allowed to spend his days with the others and his nights with us. In a way we were worried about this, as Phisit, Procet, Thani, and Y.C. had always gotten more privileges than we had, and we often wondered if they were in cahoots with the guards. Phisit was particularly under suspicion, since he didn't want to escape and had talked Y.C. into staying. The two of them insisted that we not try to escape because if we got away, the guards would kill them in retaliation. "Go to hell!" I told them. "I'm going even if I have to go alone! I'm not going to rot away the way you've done for the past three years!" Duane had argued with Phisit about the escape to the point where they weren't even on speaking terms.

The friction between the Asians and the Americans increased when we found that the guards had given Procet some medicine and he had hidden it from us. We found it under his bed of leaves between the bamboo slats. We had always shared everything with the others, but finding Procet's hidden medicine proved they were holding out on us. I was mad enough to start a fight and probably would have if Duane hadn't talked some sense into me, telling me I hadn't been around long enough to understand them.

Duane, Gene and I were now molded into one purpose—escape—and we worked on it together. The only disagreement among us was that I still thought we should get the guns and kill the whole gang, especially Little Hitler and Crazy Horse.

On rare occasions we were allowed outside. One evening we were fed some broth in a round pot. When we had finished eating and laid the pot on the ground, a small chicken jumped into it. I swung my foot toward the pot to chase the chicken off, wishing we could eat it. Windy left immediately and began jabbering with Little Hitler. We were all sitting quietly inside the hut when Little Hitler and Windy came striding over with the rest of the guards, their rifles at the ready position.

"Procet, Yerman, come!" Little Hitler ordered us out of the hut. We looked at each other, afraid and not knowing what it was all about. Procet and I came out and the guards sat us down and tied us back to back.

"What in the hell's going on?" I whispered to Procet.

"No idea."

Little Hitler, his hands perched on his hips and his legs spread apart, stuck his face into Procet's, his voice hissing with anger.

"What'd he say?" I asked, and before Procet could answer, Little Hitler smacked him sharply across the face. The guards began beating us, then pulled back and started shooting all around us. Windy's gun jammed and as he was fooling around with it, it went off, the bullets just clearing our heads. Then the guards threw us back into the hut with Gene and Duane.

Procet glared at me in anger but I still didn't know what the row was all about.

"You kicked the pot with your foot and put an evil spell on it," he said.

"Now, wait a minute. I chased the chicken out of the pot,

but I didn't kick it." I could feel myself starting to boil. "How was I supposed to know about that?"

Procet just lay there, glowering at me in silence. "Next chance I get, I'm going to kill you!" he informed me.

"Kill me? Wanna make a bet? I'm going to do you in before you get that chance, so you'd better watch out!"

We were both on the verge of an explosion, our eyes fixed on each other like dogs set to attack, when Gene, the peacemaker as usual, stopped us.

The guards were ruled by their superstitions. Windy wouldn't go to the bush alone at night unless others came along and held his hand even while he urinated, all of them scared to death that a ghost would get them. Crazy Horse went into fits and would open up with his Thompson submachine gun at some spot in the jungle where he thought a ghost was hiding. He then took a stick and danced around his hut, beating the ground and yelling and chanting, trying to drive the ghosts away. As soon as he began yelling, the rest of the guards joined him. They even went to the trouble of feeding the ghosts. Periodically, they cooked a small pot of chicken, rice, and peppers. They put most of the food into Procet's rice bowl and set it at the main entrance to the camp. The remainder of the food was placed at the heads of the various trails around the camp. In the morning, of course, all the food was gone and the guards were sure the ghosts had eaten it.

Sickness, also, was the work of ghosts. When one of the guards became sick suddenly, the others said the reason was that he had eaten the ghosts' food and the only way to save him was to drive the ghost out. They went into the victim's hut and beat him mercilessly. Then a medicine man dressed in feathers and beads came from the village. He jumped around, yelling and singing, jingling his monkey bones. If a man lived through such treatment, which happened infrequently, the Laotians said the ghosts had left the man. If he died, it was too bad, and his body was thrown into the jungle.

Our escape planning became most difficult when Phisit stopped talking to us altogether, and Procet later pulled the same stunt. From the time the Old Man arrived, we had received no news about the guards because of Procet's silence. Weeks later Procet, smiling broadly, broke his silence, acting as if there had been nothing wrong between us. He then began to bring us up to date, telling us that a Big Man, as the guards called him, had arrived a week before. We had seen this man, but didn't know why he had come. He carried a portable radio, which was a sign of very high status. Procet told us that this Big Man was here to inspect the camp and instill greater revolutionary fervor in the guards. He did most of his work at the daily self-criticism meetings.

Supposedly, these meetings were a time for the guards to confess their wrongs and make amends. Instead, they turned out to be brag sessions; no matter how bad the confessions of one guard were, the next one tried to top him. Sometimes the guards would beat us up for no reason, just so they could confess it at the next self-criticism meeting. After the criticisms, the Big Man would give the guards pep talks, telling them what great fighters the Laotian men were, the best in the world. He told them that Laos was the wealthiest country in the world, that all of the food and gold attracted the French, and that the Americans were thieves. The more he talked, the louder he became and finally he would be screaming and yelling, the guards imitating him and waving their weapons in the air.

The guards believed everything the Big Man told them. If he said the way to find salt was to dig a hole in the ground, the guards would start digging. When that turned up nothing, they moved over a few yards and dug another hole. When they found nothing there, they grew angry and blamed the lack of salt on the Americans. They even believed they were the wealthiest country in the world, never stopping to question the fact that everyone was on the verge of starvation. For years, their leaders had been telling them that their government wouldn't let them down, that there would be rice. "I believe it," I told Gene. "Pretty soon they'll walk in with a big sack with U.S.A. on it, just like on their ammunition belts and blankets. Then they'll say it was the U.S. who stole it from them in the first place."

Procet told us that Y.C. was still saving rice, which was really surprising. Y.C. had been saying he was going to stay behind, but apparently he was planning to go along with us. His rice-saving was foolhardy, however. We had stopped saving rice because there were too many close calls with the guards. Now Y.C. was jeopardizing the whole escape plan. Gene was on the best terms with Y.C., and he promised to talk with him about it. Procet said that even if Y.C. had changed his mind, Phisit was definitely going to stay behind. Phisit was afraid that he'd get out and then die of a malaria attack—which we all had periodically—in the middle of the jungle.

With Procet talking to us again, we were able to stop planning in secret and start making some definite decisions. We still didn't know precisely what we'd do once we were beyond the walls, but we couldn't merely hole up somewhere. The Pathet Lao were excellent trackers and they'd nail us for sure if we didn't get well ahead of them and keep moving. Floating was still the best idea—hiding by day and traveling by night. If we could get to the Big Muddy, the Mekong, it would be only a matter of time before the current would carry us into South Vietnam. Our best bet would be to steal a native raft. If that didn't work out, we had to be ready to build one ourselves.

Procet suggested that banana trees made good rafts. I was skeptical at first, but Gene and Duane agreed that banana trees did make good, easy-to-build rafts, except that they rotted away in a matter of days. We kept this idea in mind since we didn't have a machete to cut down the hard bamboo. Gene had a small blade, about two or three inches long, but it was nearly worthless because there was no handle to it. In the yard, Gene found a spent rifle cartridge and that gave him a bright idea: he could make a knife by setting the blade into the neck of the cartridge and binding the two pieces of metal with hot lead, melted from toothpaste tubes. Gene asked me for the tube where I'd hidden my money. With my tool and die maker experience, I knew that the metals wouldn't stick together, but Gene was a stubborn fellow and once he'd made up his mind about something, there was no changing it.

The problem now was to build some kind of a forge for melting the metal. The next time we were let out, I scooped up some mud from the edge of the latrine and with it I was able to fashion a little stove. We tried to make a fire by rubbing two pieces of bamboo together, but we were far too weak to rub for any length of time.

With the Big Man around, the guards tried to stay awake all night smoking their bamboo pipes. Their tobacco was very low grade and to keep it lit they always had a smoldering stick or two nearby. The burnt end of the stick was good charcoal, so we scrounged for these sticks and saved them. Then, to start our fire, a Thai called out to the guards for a light. One of them would come over with a smoldering stick. We would stick a homemade pipe through the door and suck on it like mad while the guard held the glowing end of the stick to the top of the bowl. The hard sucking nauseated me and I figured the tobacco must have been at least half dope. With the three of us taking turns sucking on the pipe, we kept it burning long enough to transfer the glowing tobacco onto a piece of charcoal. Once the charcoal started to glow, we stuck it into the mud stove and fanned it with an oak-leaf fan that Y.C. had once given Duane as a present. The tiny bed of coals was smokeless and the guards never found out about it.

Knife-making proved to be a boondoggle for Gene. He'd get the metal just hot enough to run, but when it was time for him to pour it, it would already be hard.

"Maybe next time," I kept telling him, but even he realized it was futile. "I'll swipe a machete for you instead," I told him, trying to make him feel better.

"Yeah, okay," he said. He was obviously upset that it hadn't worked but said he'd give it another try. Even if it didn't work, it gave us something to do.

Sometimes Gene asked me if I wanted a sip from his glass of beer. He described it in every detail to tantalize us—a tall glass, cool, and filled with frothy pilsener beer, water droplets slinking down the sides—until we begged him to stop. Duane's thing was 19-cent hamburgers. He'd worked for McDonald's while he was going to college and had practically lived on cheap hamburgers. My specialty was noodles and Spam. Gene hated Spam but said that if he got out he was going to send me a whole case of it.

Our talk was also about freezers. We would stack them with the most delicious food a man could imagine. I had never met a pie-eater, but after listening to Gene describe the pies he had eaten and planned to eat, I vowed that when I got back I would have pie for dessert every night. I told them about the Farmer's Market in San Francisco and how I used to go down right before it closed to buy tomatoes or cucumbers at cut rates. I had visions of buying whole case-lots of tomatoes and cucumbers and storing them against slack times, but Duane told me that tomatoes and cucumbers didn't freeze well. After a while these food conversations grew too painful. Many times one or all of us would sit and cry, thinking of food and home and the future. Everything good was so far away, everything nearby was so bleak and getting worse.

Malay, the camp dog, had become very important to us. Because of the lack of protein in our diets, any cuts or sores we had healed very slowly, if at all. We found, however, that if Malay licked them, the cuts would begin to heal. Like all the village curs, he was a mean, untrustworthy dog, but when he found out we meant him no harm, he became our friend. Sometimes he spent hours sitting in front of our hut just looking in. The guards, on the other hand, really took advantage of him. Malay was a good hunter, particularly for snakes. He didn't stray too far into the jungle and stayed close enough to the camp to summon the guards when he found a good-sized snake. Sometimes he became overzealous and attacked a snake too big for him. Several times the guards had to free him from a constrictor that had coiled around him. The guards rarely shared any of the prize with Malay, which was unfair to him as he was the best hunter in the camp, catching far more snakes than the guards ever did with their fancy traps. They even beat Malay when they caught him scrounging food from their pots. One time the normally peaceful Jumbo lost his temper and threw his machete at Malay. The blade laid half his head open. He was so badly hurt he couldn't even bark. He managed to crawl off and hide in a place near our hut where we would see him. We were sure he'd be dead by morning, but the next day he was still blinking his eyes, the wound oozing something that looked like brain tissue. Procet bandaged him as best he could. We were sure he would die each night, but somehow he made it. Only a few weeks later he was out running around in the jungle like a new dog.

The shortage of food put us all on edge. Little Hitler worked out his anger at the Old Man by blaming his troubles on us. He told the rest of the guards to beat us and shoot us if we offered even the least resistance. He made no exceptions—the get-tough policy applied to the Asians as well as to the Americans. Phisit was worried by this, as he'd always gotten along well with the guards and had been given special favors. But the guards were getting desperate. Phisit now knew that if they decided to eliminate us, he wouldn't be spared. He agreed to escape with us on one condition: that we steal guns and be prepared to shoot the guards if need be. I agreed immediately because that was what I had wanted to do all along, but the others were still skeptical.

Sprinkles fell from time to time but not the torrents we were expecting. I had been sure I'd be free by May 22, but finally the big day came—my twenty-eighth birthday. The guys wished me the best and toasted me with our awful drinking water. But still no rain, and we were sad.

The next day a guard told Little Hitler that we refused to put on the handcuffs. This was the chance Little Hitler had been looking for, and he came marching into our hut with the guards, all armed, and began to talk incessantly. Idiot was, of course, lying through his teeth. We could get out of cuffs so easily there was no reason for us to resist them, but we couldn't exactly explain this to Little Hitler. After his speech he aimed his automatic weapon first at Duane, then at Y.C. and at Procet, playing with the trigger the whole time. I was back against the wall, out of sight and safe for the moment. The guards urged Little Hitler to shoot. Crazy Horse raised his M-1 and without reason or warning fired into the ground, exciting and agitating the whole group. All the while Little Hitler kept the gun on Procet, staring at him coldly over the sights. Procet was whispering something to him. Little Hitler then pulled the trigger. We all heard the firing pin fall, but there was no explosion. The chamber of his rifle had been empty.

The other guards thought his game an ingenious idea, and all of them began taunting us. Some of them took the cartridges out of the chamber of their guns, pointed the guns at one of us, then fired, letting the pin fall on the empty chamber. Others left their guns loaded and played with the triggers. It was nerve-racking to sit there tied up while some idiot who didn't know beans about handling a weapon pointed a loaded gun at your forehead and played with the trigger. When they were done with their little game, they secured our shackles and left, shouting and laughing.

We didn't have much to say to each other that night. But the experience had the effect of solidifying our escape plans. Duane said he would go along with any plan to get out, even if it meant killing the guards. Procet seethed with rage. "Just leave me Little Hitler," he said. "I want him for myself. That's all I ask."

Phisit had been able to win special favor again with the guards by becoming their medic. The medic in our camp was a villager who knew absolutely nothing about medicine, not even elementary things like sterilizing instruments. The only medicine he had was a crate of vitamin shots one of the guards had found somewhere. Once Phisit himself fell into the medic's incompetent clutches when he was down with malaria. He insisted on giving Phisit a vitamin shot. When the medic brought out a needle that looked like a rusty nail and a rubber-topped injection bottle with its label missing, Phisit refused. Nevertheless, he got the shot and after a while his arm began to swell until there was a bump the size of a golf ball. Some of us began to think it was a type of cancer.

An infection had swollen Moron's big toe into an enormous bulb. Phisit wanted to lance the toe but Moron refused. Phisit then had him soak his foot in hot water, and when Moron wasn't looking, he inserted the needle. Moron made all sorts of ugly noises but the deed was done and complaining got him nowhere.

HOI HET: NEW HOME · 127

Phisit squeezed out the pus and powdered the incision with scrapings from his hoard of pills. Moron's toe was as good as new in no time and, from then on, Phisit replaced the medic, who was given a rifle and put on guard duty like everyone else.

One of our regular Sunday discussions was interrupted by the sound of aircraft overhead. The planes were becoming a daily occurrence. In the early morning they came up the valley toward the Mugia Pass and then about 9:00 A.M. they returned. Most of the planes were Spads, and I wondered if they would be from the *Ranger* or maybe even from my squadron, VA-145. On that particular Sunday they came in much lower than usual. Y.C. yelled that he could see them but our door faced the wrong way. Finally we caught sight of them as they passed over, and for a second I could just barely make out the green stripe and the lion of Squadron VA-145. I felt as if I had been hit hard below the belt—so close and yet so far.

We didn't talk much the rest of the day—just sat there, waiting for the sound of their return run, but they never came back.

The lack of food left us dizzy all the time and I often wondered if we would have the strength to pull off the escape, much less travel even a mile after we broke out. We lay silently in our hut most of the day because talking took too much energy.

Nighttime had become a rather gruesome ordeal. Windy had picked up a flashlight on his last rice mission, and the guards' newest trick was to pop in on us in the middle of the night and flash the light around.

I was handcuffed to Procet, who was down with a bad case of dysentery. He defecated continuously, fouling the floor and bedding nearby. Sitting there with him in the corner, dizzy from his sick fumes, and my hands spotted with his feces, I was beginning to go crazy. The waste lying around everywhere attracted the rats and ants. We were too weak to catch the rats for food and the ants became the true torment of the jungle, surpassing even the leeches and mosquitoes.

Then a miracle occurred. The Old Man arrived with a group

of men who were carrying sacks of rice. You could feel the happiness spread throughout the camp. We smelled the fire that had been lit in the kitchen, and we waited impatiently, afraid we would be forgotten. The Old Man himself came our way with a huge basket of rice. He had the cuffs taken off and allowed us outside to sit at the table. A couple of chickens had been slaughtered, which wasn't much after being divided among nineteen men, but all that rice with a little dab of chicken was a real banquet. The Old Man stood around and watched, looking rather pleased.

The Old Man had brought another old man with him, a villager whose body was finely tattooed from head to toe. We nicknamed him "Papsco." He seemed to be a good man and a powerful one. All the time we were eating, Little Hitler sulked and scowled, obviously unhappy with our special treatment. When we were finished, he ordered us put inside in our blocks. Papsco told Little Hitler that he, himself, would decide when we were to be locked up. Little Hitler shut his mouth and kept it shut.

After we had finished the first basket of rice, Gene asked for more and got another basketful. We stuffed ourselves greedily and then divided up the leftover rice for future use. We walked around the compound, using the time to clean up and empty our overflowing refuse tubes. Thani was allowed to go down to the waterhole and returned shortly with twelve full containers of rotten water which we used to wash our bodies and clothes.

After having starved so long, the large quantity of rice we ate gave us all the urge to go to the hole. Y.C. was first as usual, calling out, *"Pai tai!"* Right away Papsco told the guards to get with it, and they didn't harass us as much, letting us have the hole for as long as we liked. Once we were back inside, Phisit said that the Old Man was planning haircuts for us the next day. That meant something was up—whether good or bad, there was no way of telling.

The next afternoon, Sot brought us a pair of scissors and a block of wood that served as a barber's chair. Phisit played barber and the four of us took turns sitting on the block. Then Phisit's hands became too tired and he had to postpone the rest of the haircuts. We tried to find some use for the hair but couldn't think of any.

Sot came in with a mirror, just like the one I had stolen from Bastard, and wanted to shave our beards. Gene was first and sat on the block with his chin in the air while Sot scraped his beard off with a little knife. Occasionally Gene cried out and little red rivulets trickled down his face. Duane was the next victim but when my turn came, I refused. Through Phisit I told Sot that I would rather shave myself, giving the excuse that my beard was very tough.

Gene now looked like somebody else, not the old, bearded man I had known. His face was still sunken and white but he looked much younger. Sot lent him the mirror and Gene couldn't get over how he looked. Then he let me take a look at myself, which was a big shock. My cheekbones protruded from my own sunken face and my formerly ruddy complexion was now sallow, covered haphazardly with an ill-kept Vandyke beard.

We spent the rest of the day laying plans for escape. As we talked, I realized I'd made a mistake in not letting Sot shave me. None of the guards or villagers had beards and if we escaped soon, my hairy face would identify me immediately as an American.

Evening was just settling over us when a beautiful blue iridescent butterfly flew into our hut and settled gently on the crossbar of our door. Slowly she folded and unfolded her wings. We all held our breath, touched by the beauty of it. When she finally took flight, we remained silent for a moment, almost as if in prayer.

The beard problem was solved a few days later when Papsco gave Phisit the scissors again. But my real worry was my left arm, which had withered considerably. I massaged it every day but all of us agreed it looked hopeless. One day I was lying on my back with the elbow of my left arm on the floor and the arm straight up, trying to get some movement, when the arm did, indeed, move. "Hey, Gene, look here!" I whispered to him, afraid if I talked too loudly I might scare my arm. He shuffled over and peered at me, wondering why my voice was so cautious. Using all my strength again, I moved my wrist a little. Gene just sat there wide-eyed, his hand on his chin.

I began practicing with the arm every day. In a week I could lift my hand; in two weeks I could lift my hand twice in a row, and soon my left arm was almost as good as my right, only weaker. I was elated.

The rain was very long in coming. We already had the escape planned in minute detail and committed to memory. We agreed to escape on a moonless night. I would be the first one out, then Gene, Procet, and Duane in that order. I would go over to the other hut and open the door. Meanwhile Gene and Procet would open the gate leading out. Duane would make sure that the door to our hut was closed properly, and then dig up the machete I had stolen from Crazy Horse weeks before and buried near the corner of our hut. Thani would close and check the door to their hut. When Gene and Procet had opened the gate, Procet would feel his way along the fence and retrieve our shoes, which were hanging under the guards' hut. The others would then follow Gene and me along the fence leading toward the crapper. There my job was to make a hole in the fence, guide the others through the hole, and give them back their gear once they got through.

We couldn't leave a gaping hole in the fence because often the guards went to the latrine first thing in the morning, and a hole in the fence would surely warn them something was wrong. We had to make sure they didn't suspect anything until at least midmorning because we needed that extra two or three hours to get as far away as possible. Since the fence was tied together with old rattan that couldn't be reused, I planned to carry some rattan to put the fence back together and patch the hole. That done, I would work my way along the line of men to Gene up front and pick up the loose end of the rope attached to his waist. Our objective was the waterhole. I would move from one checkpoint to the next, giving Gene three tugs each time I reached one. He would bring the others along the rope to me; then I would go ahead to find the next checkpoint, and so on until we came to the waterhole. Once we were safely across the creek, the total darkness would prevent us from putting much distance between us and the camp, but, hopefully, in the morning we would get a lot farther away. The rain would wash out our tracks, and there would be no way for the guards to track us.

We went over and over our plans until everything was down pat. One important question remained to be answered: once they knew we were gone, how long would it take for reinforcements to join the search? We found this out by accident a few weeks later when a guard came up from the waterhole at a dead run—gasping, sputtering, and yelling at the top of his lungs until the rest of the guards had surrounded him. Moron, Jumbo, and Sot gathered up their belongings and ran off toward the village. The rest of them grabbed their rifles and threw themselves into the foxholes around the camp's perimeter. Thani soon found out that the guard had seen the print of a boot at the waterhole and was sure it had been made by an American. The guards were sure that an American guerrilla outfit was somewhere nearby and, of course, we all hoped the guards were right. One of us stayed on the lookout all the time, hoping for a sign, but our savior never came.

We did, however, find out how long it would take reinforcements to arrive. The footprints were seen about noon and on the following morning reinforcements came. The reinforcements were Viet Cong, which really surprised me because we didn't think there were any in this area. Knowing they were around was very unsettling. Everything I had heard about them was frightening—their little Chinese caps, their eyes, their curved lips, and their muscular legs. I had heard about their treatment of prisoners and was afraid they would treat us to a dose of their brutality just for fun. For two days the Viet Cong combed the entire area, finding only more footprints. All the while, Idiot's story kept getting wilder, and pretty soon he had actually seen the men, wearing shiny helmets glinting in the sunlight, as they walked past him up the creek.

This episode taught us a number of important lessons. We knew now that it would take almost a full day for the trackers to get here and begin the search. That was more time than we had hoped for. We also knew we should get a substantial distance from camp before wearing shoes, as boots left an easy trail for the trackers. Bare footprints left by an American looked much like those of a Laotian. We realized that with the Viet Cong after us, escape wasn't a playful game of cowboys and Indians. It was for keeps. But we were committed and, on some beautiful rainy night, we would be on our way.

Gene, Duane, and I often discussed what we should do once we were out of the camp, but we never shared our ideas with the Asians. Neither group trusted the other. We were sure that if they knew where we were going and one of them were recaptured, he would surely squeal loud and clear to save his own neck. So we told them nothing specific.

Gene told us that a villager in one of the camps once confided in him that he should never, never go east, since in that direction lay certain death in the impenetrable jungle. Not even the Laotians ventured into it. The villager said the only way out was west. With that in mind, we decided on our general path. We would cross at least two mountain ridges to the south, continue west in the valley beyond to the first river, float south to the East-West road, then follow the road into Thailand.

Procet and Phisit had often told us about their native country, Thailand. They emphasized the hospitality of the people, especially the monks. The monks would feed anyone and provide a place to stay because it was against their religion to ask anyone to leave. Procet urged us to contact a temple if we got into Thailand. However, we had also heard much about the Vietnamese guerrillas in northern Thailand. We decided to keep going until we reached American forces, even if it meant crawling on our hands and knees.

Slowly the weather began to change and the wind from the southwest increased. We rejoiced quietly, as this wind would bring the monsoons.

Procet stayed in our hut off and on. One evening he was lying on his bed of leaves in silence when Gene spotted Crazy Horse sneaking along the fence. In a whisper, Gene told me to check him out. I was going over to the corner to peek out and spy on Crazy Horse when I stepped over Procet. Suddenly Procet kicked me in the groin and jumped up, swinging his fists. It was over in a few seconds, since neither of us had the strength to fight, but Procet was boiling mad. He told me that stepping over someone was the worst possible taboo, and if I'd been a woman, he'd have had the right to kill me. Again he told me that he'd kill me if he ever got the chance; again I responded that he'd never get the chance and he'd better look out for his own life.

My anger refused to cool and I wanted some way to get back at Procet. The next day, while he was over with his friends in the other hut, I stole the piece of bamboo he was always playing with. In it I found more tablets in a little bottle—twenty-three in all—pills that were lifesavers in case of dysentery. I hid the tablets and later told Gene and Duane about the find. We divided the pills among us. By then I felt guilty about my theft and would have put them back if Gene had not explained how, earlier, when he was almost dying of dysentery, Procet had refused to share the pills.

One afternoon Papsco brought us a jackfruit, the yellow teat-studded fruit I'd seen hanging from the trunk of a tree when I was first shot down. I was surprised to find that the fruit was edible. The yellow insides were slimy but as sweet as honey and just as delicious. Usually only the yellow pulp is eaten, but as hungry as we were, we also ate the core. The trouble with jackfruit was that it gave us the runs.

More and more planes were flying over us every day, and it was obvious that the war was going on as strongly as ever. Bombing runs came over each morning to hit some nearby target. I was pretty sure their objective was the new road I'd been led across on the way to Par Kung. Sometimes the air was filled with the sound of a big plane, and we'd catch sight of a C-123 *Provider* cargo plane with its back door open, probably for an airdrop to some guerrilla band. We could also hear the *Dragon Wagons* (DC-3s) and the sound of their Gatling guns, the big Vulcan cannons.

With all the airplanes flying over, I wished I still had my survival mirror and radio. If I'd known when I was shot down that the Laotians regarded the body below the belt as taboo, I could have hidden my things there, and they never would have been discovered.

As we were talking about how easy it would be to signal an airplane, a frog croaked underneath the floor. We pulled up the floor and peered into the dark. The frog made a jump that cost him his life. He was only a little fellow, so we divided him very carefully. Gene found the heart and laid claim to it. At home on the farm when there was a chicken for dinner, he always had eaten the heart. The heart was no bigger than a pinhead but he said he could still taste it and was very pleased.

9 FINAL PLANS

Even though we had the mechanics of the escape down pat, the issue of how we'd group ourselves for the long trek was constantly in debate. Before my arm had started to improve, I wanted to go alone because I thought I'd be a burden on the others. However, with my arm improving gradually, I knew I would be able to pull my own weight. Procet thought we should be two groups of three, with at least one American in each group. Y.C. disagreed and wanted us all to go together. Nobody else liked that idea so Y.C. changed his mind, proposing that he, Procet, and I go together. He pointed out that Procet's guerrilla experience in Malaya would be invaluable and that, since I was jumpy and always on the go, I'd keep the other two moving even when they were tired. I balked immediately.

"It'd never work, Y.C.," I said. "Hell, we can't get along even here. How're we going to do it out there when the going gets really rough?" I wanted to go with Gene and Duane because we got along so well.

Y.C. was insistent—he wanted to have an American with him. He was afraid they might make an air contact and the pilot would refuse to pick them up because they didn't look like Americans.

"Don't be stupid," Duane said. "When you're flying a helicopter, you have a hard enough time just seeing somebody on the ground, much less telling what nationality he is. You make an S.O.S. or a distress signal and you'll get picked up, that's for sure."

However, we first had to get out, and our luck with that didn't seem to be getting any better.

The late rains were a problem not only for us but also for the Laotians. A villager Gene had met years earlier was passing through this part of the country and stopped to see Gene when he heard he was at Hoi Het. The villager told him the drought had become so bad that the people had actually begun to eat their stocks of rice seed. If they ate all the seed, famine would be their lot for sure. He asked Gene what the people could do to improve things. Gene asked our opinions but all we could suggest was to have the villagers write to Souvana Phouma and tell him of their plight. It was very poor advice, however, since none of the villagers could read or write. The villager said he was carrying a leaflet that had been dropped from a friendly plane, and Gene asked to see it. The villager had barely gotten it through the door when Little Hitler spotted him chatting with Gene and, true to his malevolent form, he scolded the villager into leaving the camp immediately. We took a close look at the leaflet and found it carried more than thirty pictures of North Vietnamese regular officers who had defected to the south. The text listed the names of the turncoat soldiers and urged all other Communist fighters to lay down their arms and stop this senseless war.

The rain didn't come and didn't come. One day I collapsed for no particular reason. I knew that if this slow rotting away went on much longer, we'd never make it past the gate. I began urging the escape once more, only now I wanted to forget the monsoons and just kill all the guards. Phisit liked the idea but Gene was reluctant, at first. But as he rolled it around in his mind, his conviction grew. "Hell, yes!" he exclaimed. We still had to convince Procet, Thani, and Y.C., which was difficult because Procet kept saying that I was being stubborn and had to take the others into consideration. I was tired of convincing and tired of dying in stages, day by day. The others could go hang themselves—I was getting out!

Duane also became committed to escape no matter what the method, an indication of just how desperate he'd become. Sometime earlier he'd asked to be transferred to Hanoi. Now he was glad that the request had been denied. Conditions were certainly better in the north, but with the well-trained North Vietnamese guards, escape was impossible. Here conditions were appalling, but we had a chance of getting away from the lackadaisical and ignorant Laotians.

Duane and I decided to make our try before July 4. On that day we would either be free or dead.

I began to look for a way out of our hut to the main fence. I started loosening the logs by digging away the dirt into which they set. Y.C. didn't like my digging, saying it was all too easy for the guards to catch me at it. I agreed that it was a risk but one we had to take. I kept on working, and soon I could tell that Y.C. was afraid he'd wake up one morning and find the rest of us gone. Gradually, as he, Procet, and Thani saw that Duane and I were going whether they came along or not, they decided to go along with our plan to steal the guards' guns and kill them.

We started planning all over again. The first thing we did was to build a model of the camp with twigs and sticks. We made it very carefully, forgetting no detail, no matter how small. Then we watched the guards like hawks and recorded every single move they made. In a matter of days we knew where every weapon was and what routine each guard followed.

The constant aircraft activity worried us. We knew that sooner or later the camp was going to be spotted. One day the sound of a plane right overhead brought us to attention. We all pressed our heads against the door and caught a glimpse of an L-19, a small plane just a little bigger than a Piper Cub. He made a turn and headed directly for us, starting a circle at about one thousand feet. He circled three or four times before disappearing. The plane alarmed the guards and sent them scurrying for their foxholes. They held their fire, however, probably because they feared they would give away their position.

I was almost certain that the L-19 was a forward air controller, and I was sure the pilot was radioing back to base that he had spotted what could be a supply dump. I urged an escape for that night, which meant giving up the idea of shooting the guards and also forcing us to escape without the cover of rain.

The alternative, with the possibility of being napalmed, sent chills down my spine.

We put it to a vote and I lost. They decided to take their chances and wait it out, thinking that escape before we were ready was too chancy. I had to agree in a way, and even though the idea of being bombed didn't exactly appeal to me, I almost hoped the Spads would come, just to prove I had been right.

As we lay there that night, with the threat of attack, we attempted conversation.

"Hey, you guys, do you realize that not one guy escaped during the Korean War?" Duane said.

"Nah, you're kidding!" That just didn't seem believable.

"Darn right," Duane assured me. "They kept telling us that over and over at survival school."

"Now, can you imagine what it would mean if we all made it out?" I said.

"We'd better make it out," interjected Procet.

"Maybe we'll be invited to President Johnson's ranch for a barbecue. Think of it!" For a moment we were all silent, wrapped up in a reverie of rare roast beef cut into thick slabs, all runny with juice. "Hell, all the astronauts do is fly around up there and everything is controlled on the ground," I told Duane and Gene. "If they got a parade, just think of what we'll get!"

"Gee, I never thought of that," Duane said. "Maybe we'll even get the Medal of Honor."

We had never before thought of the rewards that escape might bring. Now we lay there, like condemned men voicing their last wishes. Freedom was its own reward, but the idea of special recognition, maybe even from the president, added sweetness to our tasteless existence.

The next day we waited and waited for the sound of incoming planes. They never came. We were glad we hadn't decided to escape, after all, since the guards would have been close on our heels. Duane and Gene said nothing, but Y.C., Procet, and Phisit kept reminding me that I'd guessed wrong.

I knew that once we got out Duane would be a good man to have along. He was slow, so slow it took an eternity for him just to turn around, but that slowness was his strong point. I was pushy and impetuous. I might grow careless and walk right across a trail, while Duane would crawl a mile on his hands and knees to avoid one. In fact, when he was shot down, he was much more successful at avoiding the enemy than I'd been. The moment he eased up on his caution by walking along a trail, they caught him.

One day the guards formed up and marched toward the village, with Crazy Horse at the head of the column. They ordered the villagers to give them their very last pig. Crazy Horse offered what money the guards had, which was a sham because the money was worthless and the villagers knew it. When the villagers balked at trading meat for paper, Crazy Horse cocked his weapon and brandished it until they relented. The guards then marched back to the camp with a small black pig and let it run free. They nearly lost it when it hightailed back to the village. Then they tied it inside our camp about ten feet from us. In no time the pig became a miserable nuisance. It spent the whole day wallowing in its own dirt, and the fumes made us dizzy. We waited and waited for them to slaughter the pig so we might get some meat and be rid of the smell, but the time passed and the pig stayed where he was, living in his own ever-growing pile of manure.

In the evenings an aircraft that sounded like a C-130 turboprop would fly in from the south at about two thousand feet, circle our camp once or twice, then head up north, to return a few hours later. His pattern of coming and going became so habitual that it seemed sensible to plan our escape around a contact with him.

We'd been watching the guards and the camp carefully, and we knew where everything was and what each of them did every minute of the day. The only time the guards were separated from their weapons was at mealtime. They would leave their guns in their huts, walk to the kitchen, pick up the food in their turtle shells, and return to their huts. The whole trip took just about two and a half minutes. We were fortunate that the tall bamboo fence around the prison huts cut off most of the view from the kitchen. I drew up a plan of escape that made use of this short period.

We planned to leave through the bottom of the hut. I had already dug the logs out and replaced them so they could be removed quickly and easily. The first man out would make it to the fence, go through it, scramble to the guards' hut just beyond, and get the weapons—all in less than two and a half minutes. With the guns, we could take the place over without firing a shot. In fact, not firing a shot was the key to our success. If the villagers heard a gun go off, they would assume a deer had been killed and come trooping in after their share, only to stumble across our breakout.

At first the scheme sounded impossibly daring—the captives capturing the captors—but the more we talked about it, the better it sounded. We began working out the details of the plan, step by careful step. First of all, we could count on getting only three weapons in the guards' hut. Since some of us wouldn't have guns at the beginning, we had to be sure that the men who were armed would use the weapons correctly. If trouble started, they would have to act quickly without fear. Y.C. and Thani were ruled out immediately, as Y.C. couldn't handle a rifle at all and Thani knew just enough to be dangerous. Neither Duane nor Gene liked the idea of being involved in any possible shooting, so that left Phisit, Procet, and me with the guns. That posed a problem since we had to have Phisit in our hut on the big day.

I would go first and Phisit and Procet would follow at my signal, once I opened the hole in the fence. Duane and Gene would come out next. Gene would go to the corner of the compound farthest from the hut, while Duane would meet Phisit and Procet, who would then be armed by me. Duane, Phisit, and Procet would slip carefully along the fence toward Papsco's hut, and Duane on signal would leap into it, grab the carbine, and keep the Old Man quiet. In the meantime, Procet and Phisit would run into the open to where they had a clear view of the kitchen. During the time Phisit, Procet, and Duane made their way toward the kitchen, I would run up to Gene and around the corner of the stockade to a bamboo cluster near one of the guards' huts. A Thompson submachine gun was kept there. Gene would jump into the hut and use that vantage point to cover me, and I would then run out toward the kitchen. Phisit and Duane would hold the guards in the kitchen at gun-point while Procet, Gene, and I would collect hand grenades and rifles. Procet and Gene would use a grenade to set a booby trap a little way down on the trail from the camp, a rifle tied to it as bait. Anyone coming up the trail would pick up the rifle and set off the device, killing himself and warning us. Procet and Gene would be hiding near their trap and would shoot any Pathet Lao or capture any villagers that came along. While Procet and Gene were setting up their booby trap, Thani, Phisit, and I would be tying up the guards. Y.C. and Duane would search all the huts, piling everything of value on the porch of the Old Man's hut next to the kitchen, and dividing the hoard equally among us.

While Duane and Y.C. were scouring the camp, Phisit and I would drag the guards one by one into the bush, strangle them, and throw the corpses into the foxholes on the perimeter of the camp. We planned to keep Papsco, the Old Man, and Crazy Horse alive. Nobody had the heart to kill the two old men, and Crazy Horse was the smartest guard in the lot, who knew the country well and where the friendlies and the enemies were. We planned to pump all the information we could out of him. If we didn't make air contact with the C-130, we would use the three of them as hostages.

We would gather up all the food we could find to hold us through our wait. Y.C. would catch the guards' two chickens and kill them, slaughter the pig and cook it, but let Malay live. We figured we would stay in camp and try to make air contact for four days and, if that failed, we would have to begin traveling on foot.

We would immediately try to contact the C-130 that was making the habitual evening visits. We planned to make a pile of bamboo, laced with tinder, and place it close to the small cooking fire for the pig. It could then be lit at the first sound of the C-130. Once the fire and the smoke had attracted the pilot's attention, we would signal him. If it was still light enough, we'd lay out an S.O.S. with the guards' tan mosquito nets. If it was dark, three of us would wave long sticks, the ends glowing from the fire, in the pattern of an S.O.S., each taking one letter. At the same time Y.C., who had been a radio operator for Air America and knew Morse Code backward and forward, would try to send a message by covering and uncovering a pot filled with glowing coals. The message he'd send would be: "Rescue—Free prisoners—Free prisoners—Dieter Dengler." We agreed upon my name because I was last to be shot down and would be the easiest to verify.

It was a good plan. All we needed was the right chance to pull it off. As we put the final polish on the plan, Little Hitler left on a rice mission. Before leaving, he appeared at our door and demanded my ring. I told him I'd lost it down the crapper, but he didn't believe me. He promised that if I didn't produce the ring when he got back, things would go badly for me. He stopped back again a few minutes later and I gave him the ring without argument. We hoped very much that he would make it back before the escape, since we all looked forward to doing him in.

Killing the guards was one thing; in fact, it seemed fairly simple. But we debated for a long time about killing anyone else we encountered. The jungle has many eyes and ears, and if we let anyone go out of the goodness of our hearts, word of our presence could get around in a matter of minutes. When it came to a choice between my life and theirs, I would have to take the other guy's every time. Duane said he'd evade the issue by avoiding people. The others weren't sure what they would do in the case of women and children, but they all agreed that if they bumped into a soldier or a man looking like one, they'd kill him without hesitation.

The food situation was again very critical. The only protein we'd seen in several weeks was a bucket of tadpoles the Old Man had caught. He had mashed the little black wigglers into a slimy mess and even though we were used to eating stinking dead rats and maggots, mashed tadpoles were hard to swallow, literally and figuratively.

One thing we really dreaded about the prospect of traveling

in the jungle was the leeches. We had to find some way to keep those black bastards off us. As an experiment, we stretched a leech out on a twig, fixing him so he couldn't crawl away, then laid him out in the sunlight. We were sure the sun would cook him to a shriveled crisp in no time but when we released him, he crawled away as if nothing had happened. After more experimenting, we found that the best leech repellent was tobacco. Straight, concentrated tobacco juice killed them in a matter of seconds. We made little pouches to fit around our knees and filled them with the tobacco that Phisit had bribed from the guards in exchange for his medical services. Our idea was that the rain would keep the tobacco soaked, and the juice would run down our legs and discourage the leeches.

One evening Thani overheard the guards discussing our fate. They proposed shooting us, dragging our bodies into the jungle, and making it look as if they had shot us trying to escape. Our deaths would allow them to go home to get some food, and would earn the praise of the Big Man. They all liked the idea immensely.

Thani told Phisit, who in turn told Procet, who told us. "That's it!" I told them. "That's the signal. I'm not waiting around here for any more voting. I'm getting out of this joint."

They all nodded their heads in agreement. We set the date for the next day or the day after, while Little Hitler and nine other guards were gone, leaving only nine including Papsco and the Old Man, who didn't really count. That meant seven prisoners versus seven guards, even odds for once. I still hoped Little Hitler would show up alone, as I wanted to see his face when he saw us with weapons. And I wanted to hear him beg for his life! However, I knew I had to keep my head and not jeopardize the escape with my desire to kill him.

We were let out that afternoon for five minutes to eat some rice broth. While the rest sat around the table, I slipped behind our hut, pretending to take a leak. Instead, I tried the logs and bamboo pieces I had loosened to make certain they had not resettled in the ground. They moved easily. Everything else was ready.

After we were all back inside, Nook came into our yard and

threw the pig a corncob. The kernels had been eaten away and only the small shriveled cob remained. I raked it over to our door, and by using two sticks I managed to get it inside. It was filthy from the pig's manure, but I was starving and was going to eat it anyway. The next thing I knew, Moron came running over, yelling at the top of his lungs and pointing his rifle at my face. I crawled into my corner and the others lay flat on their bellies.

"Dieter," Procet whispered to me. "Moron wants you to come out."

"He'll kill me!"

Moron said something to Procet and Procet translated: "He said he won't shoot you."

Before I even got to the door, Moron had it open and took hold of me. He put me in my footblock and dragged me outside into the yard, where the rest of the guards had assembled. My heart was pounding and I could feel the watching eyes of the guys in the huts. Moron waved the corncob in my face, then threw it back to the pig. "So that's it," I thought, "we're even less than pigs." They beat me, then threw me back inside, after which I just sat staring out of the hut. Procet broke the silence by saying, "Don't forget, kick them in the head so they'll rot in hell."

Even without my beating, the escape plan had to be changed at the last minute. Y.C. had suddenly fallen ill with a type of attack he'd suffered once before, about a year earlier. He could barely move his legs, and the pain was very bad. Our grouping had been set up but Procet told him that taking him along with them would be suicide. Y.C. said nothing, nor did any of the rest of us. I knew Procet was right. We hardly had enough strength to support our own weight, much less anyone else's. Even if Y.C.'s legs got better, he would still slow them down considerably. Unless we made air contact with the C-130 from the camp, there was no hope for him. It was a terrible conclusion. We all groped for the right words, afraid to condemn a fellow man to death to save our own skins.

Finally Gene spoke up in anger. "Y.C., you're going with me! Don't listen to that damned Procet. Procet, you go to hell!"

FINAL PLANS · 145

"No," Y.C. said quietly, "thanks, but no thanks. He's right —you'll never make it out with me along."

"The hell! We'll make it. Anyway your legs might just get better."

"By tomorrow? You don't believe that," he told Gene. "If your legs are okay, we'll still take you with us," Procet added.

Y.C., however, knew a fairweather friend when he saw one, and snapped, "Not on your life. I'll never go with you guys. Never." Then Y.C. turned toward Gene and very calmly said, "Gene, if you mean it, we'll go together." As Y.C. spoke, he watched Gene's eyes for a rebuff. There was none, and Gene said, "You bet!"

10 ESCAPE

No one said anything, and my mind raced with questions and worries. As it was, the three Thais were better adapted to survive in this jungle than we were. Phisit had been a paratrooper in Malaysia and he really knew the jungle well. With the added burden of Y.C., we three Americans were now at a real disadvantage. I waited until the three of us were alone in our own hut to bring up the topic again.

"Gene, we just can't do it," I told him. He remained silent.

"Leave him be, Dieter," Duane said.

"Nah, he's right," Gene said, "so we don't go with the two of you."

"Don't be a fool—we want you with us," I said.

"And I want Y.C." Gene's determination was unwavering. Though the darkness hid his face from me, I could tell that he was worried but also dead set on his plan.

"Listen, you guys," he said, "Y.C. and I will go together by ourselves and then after we make it over the one ridge, we'll lie in wait for air contact. Y.C. has his white shirt to use for signaling and we'll have enough food. I'm sure we'll make it. If you guys make it out before we do, be sure someone looks for us, and tell him where to look. Okay?"

For a while all three of us remained silent, then began to chatter in our usual way. We were all nervous and sleep did not come easily. Tomorrow we would be alive and free—or dead.

In the morning I didn't want to wake up. I'd slept well in spite of the thought of escape, and I wanted to cling to sleep a little longer. Gene rousted me out. "The C-130—it flew over again last night!"

That was good news. "Man," I said, "if it comes over tonight, we're home free."

The Old Man let us out for a few minutes. While the others were milling about, I went around to the latrine behind our hut, dug up the stolen machete buried there and got it back into the hut without Nook seeing me.

After we were put back inside, the day dragged intolerably, minute by minute. The more I thought about the escape, the more it scared me. Was it the right thing to do? Should we wait until more of the guards were gone? If anything went wrong, we'd all be killed. Was the slim chance of freedom worth the high risk of death? No matter how bad the conditions were in the camp, at least I was still alive. The moment I committed myself to escape I gave up that firm grip on life. I knew that as soon as we were on the other side of that fence and into the jungle, the rest would be up to us. It would have been so much easier and more secure to stay where we were and give it another six months or a year, hoping the war would end and we'd be released.

Duane was sitting by the door looking out.

"What're you thinking?" I asked him.

"That tomorrow we'll be free men!"

That did it for me. From then on I tried to think only positively.

Phisit came over to our hut after getting permission from the Old Man. He brought Y.C.'s can along. Gene took down the bamboo containers full of rice and we used the can to measure out each man's portion. The rats had been into one container and little bugs crawled around in the rest, but there was more rice than we thought there'd be and it was all hard and dry. We gave Gene an extra portion since he was going to lay low with Y.C. and would probably spend more time in the jungle than we would. We put on our escape clothes. Gene got his rucksack ready while Duane gave his hat a last greening with leaves. We pushed my bed of leaves aside and lifted the light mat covering the hole. We pried the bamboo pieces a little farther apart and tied them back with some rattan so that the hole was wide enough for a man to get through easily.

The sky looked great, not a cloud in sight, and we were sure we would make air contact. That thought alone kept us going. I felt like screaming out loud, just to settle the butterflies in my stomach.

Almost as if they knew what was happening, Moron came over to our hut and just stood outside looking in, while Phisit and I pretended to be playing on a makeshift chess board. Moron stood there for close to an hour and my heart was going a few beats too fast all the while. "Damn it, why doesn't he leave!" I said under my breath to Phisit. Procet was pretending to sleep in the darkest corner of the hut but actually was hiding a couple of containers of rice under his shirt. I was sure that despite the bad light the guard could see that we were wearing different clothes. We'd worn these clothes a few times before to accustom the guards to the change, but I wasn't at all sure that the ruse had worked. I felt a foreboding—that he must have known we were up to something.

Phisit said something to Moron, then faked a smile as he said to me, "I told Moron to move a piece, so act worried, as if his move hurt you."

I scowled at Moron's dumb, random move, pretending to be losing the game. I moved and Moron quickly countered.

"Good boy," Phisit said, and I didn't know if he meant me or Moron.

After a few more moves, I gave a deep sigh and shook my head, throwing my hands up in defeat. "You won!" Phisit told Moron.

With a wide, silly grin spreading over his stupid face, Moron nodded his head, awed by the whole thing, and strode off hooking his thumb under the rifle sling on his shoulder. My heart was still pounding and both Gene and Duane had turned a shade whiter. "Good thinking, Phisit," I said.

Thani was keeping a constant eye on the guards as Y.C. called to us, "The guards are in the kitchen."

"But chow time hasn't been called!" I said. It was too early for them to be there. Was it a trap?

"They're probably hungry, like us," Gene said. That seemed logical enough and I dismissed my negative thought.

We all looked at each other. The moment had come. Duane brought out the water container and filled our cups. "To freedom!" we toasted. "To freedom, dead or alive!" I thought to myself.

I let myself down through the hole and crouched under our hut. While I waited for the word that all of the guards were in the kitchen, I worked my way to the logs I'd loosened previously and began removing the dirt. Then I heard: "All in the kitchen."

This was it. I grabbed the logs, lifted them out and laid them down alongside the hut. I bellied out to the fence and started to work on it. Then I heard Phisit mumble and I knew that something had already gone wrong. My body worked faster than I could think. In a split second I crawled back under the hut, sloppily replaced the poles and climbed up through the hole, putting my mat and leaves in place and flopping on top of them. My face was flushed and my heart was pumping hard, the blood pounding at my temples, as Phisit sat there just as calm as could be.

"What the hell is going on?" I demanded between breaths.

"Two of the guards were missing," Phisit said, with no hint of excitement in his voice. "I didn't think we should do it."

Anger came out of me like steam, exploding from a safety valve. Here was the second man deciding at the last moment that it was too risky, but waiting until my ass was on the line to let me know about it. I was in a murderous mood. "Damn you, Phisit, if you ever pull that again, I'll keep going and get a gun and come in and let you have it, believe me!" I was boiling mad now and he knew there was nothing idle about my threat.

We just finished putting the rice back into the hollow roof poles when Nook walked up with a bowl of rice broth. He let us out to sit at the table. When he left, I slipped around the hut and finished the job of replacing the logs and fastening the bamboo poles. I sat down at my place and noticed that the rest of them had hardly touched their broth. Out of spite, I ate all of mine. Without looking my way, Phisit left the table and went back to his own hut.

We were locked up for the night and the blocks and cuffs seemed more unbearable than usual, a cruel reminder of the imprisonment we seemed incapable of escaping. It was a miserable evening. I kept thinking how close I had come to being killed. Then we found out from eavesdropping on the guards that the two missing men, the ones Phisit was so worried about, had left to spend the night in the village. Phisit's supposed problem wasn't a problem at all, only an advantage, as the odds would have been five to seven, in our favor. Almost as if to rub it in, the C-130 circled over the camp several times. We resolved we would try again tomorrow and would succeed. Then we fell silent. I stared at the ceiling without seeing it, my mind far away —thinking of Marina, of my parents and friends, and freedom.

Morning came and we readied ourselves for the escape in near silence. We divided the rice and changed our clothes once more. Phisit grew worried and cautious again. He thought that the guards knew we were up to something.

"Maybe we should wait until tomorrow?" he suggested.

"Not on your life," I replied, giving him a dirty look.

We watched carefully to see if the guards would keep their weapons with them. As long as they parked the guns as usual in their hut, the escape was on.

At about 4:00 P.M. we took our footblocks off. We sat around, waiting for the word to come from Thani and Y.C. in the other hut. Thani again kept the watch, relating what he saw to Y.C., who would then call out in a hushed voice to Duane who was stationed at the door of our hut.

"Guards entering kitchen," Y.C. called.

"Guards entering kitchen," Duane repeated.

"Don't have weapons," Y.C. informed Duane who repeated it.

"Great," I whispered to our group. "We'll have them. It's on."

Y.C. mumbled something. "What did he say?" we asked.

"All in the kitchen, but one's missing!" Duane said.

I knew if we were ever going to go, we had to go now. "Hell, let's go. He's probably not back from the village, yet," I said. Gene, Phisit, and Procet agreed. Duane said it was okay and called back, "It's on."

With the practice of the previous day's false start, I was confident I could go even faster this time. I let myself down under the hut, pulled out the two loosened logs and crawled out. I glanced back and saw Phisit's head and shoulders coming through the opening. I untied the rattan holding the fence together and slipped the cross-hatched bamboo pieces upward to make a hole through which to crawl.

There was no fear now. Like a cat, I jumped up to the porch of the guards' hut and made my way across it, the bamboo poles squeaking uneasily at my every step as I let myself in through the side entrance. There were two Chinese weapons leaning against the wall. Then I spotted an American M-1 in the far corner. I looked out through the front entrance of the hut and realized I was standing in full view of the kitchen, about a hundred feet away. I jerked myself back against the wall, and when no one was looking, I jumped across the open doorway to the M-1 on the other side. I heard Duane's name called, the signal for him to leave the hut and join Procet and Phisit. I grabbed a full ammunition belt and ran across the hut and out onto the porch. Without stopping, I tossed the two Chinese rifles toward Procet and Phisit, then jumped to the ground, checking my M-1 to make sure it was loaded.

So far, everything was working as planned and even going faster than we had anticipated. Less than a minute had passed. Phisit, Procet, and Gene were already in position and Duane was running toward the two Thais. I ran after and past Gene and he quickly followed me to the bamboo cluster, where we waited for a few seconds.

A noise on the other side of the compound indicated that Phisit and Procet were moving out of their hiding place. I ran out from the cluster as Gene took off for the second guards' hut to get the Thompson submachine gun and to cover me from the side door. The kitchen was in full view now and I yelled, "*Yute, yute!*"

The world turned over before my shout had stopped echoing. We had expected the guards to be so surprised by the attack that they would just sit there, stunned, and let us take over without a fight. But just before my shout, they all started to run toward me. They must have seen Procet and Phisit on the other side just before I yelled. They had gone about fifteen feet when a shot rang out and I felt the air swish past my head. I hadn't expected any of them to have a rifle and the near miss seemed unreal. I then realized that it had to be the missing guard or Papsco. Our plan to take the place over without firing a shot had gone right down the drain.

Screaming and yelling filled the air. Someone was shooting wildly in my direction, and I wondered what had happened to the other guys, especially Gene, who was supposed to be covering me from the hut. I seemed to be all alone, out in the open.

Only three feet away, Moron was coming on at a full gallop, his machete cocked high over his head. I fired from the hip point-blank into him. The force of the blast hung him in the air, his machete still raised, and then spun him backwards to the ground. There was blood gushing from a huge hole in his back. I stood over him with my mouth wide open, amazed that a single slug could do such damage and mindful of nothing but the horrible-looking back.

Screams and shots snapped me back to reality. I spun around just in time to see Nook trying to outflank me. "Damn you, Gene! Where the hell is everybody?" I yelled into the air as I fired at Nook. The bullet hit him in the side and he collapsed, still yelling at the top of his lungs. I shot again to finish him off, but he kept on yelling.

The guards were running every which way now and I opened up at the fleeting forms. I saw one man drop, and then everything became a confused blur. I reloaded my M-1 and through it all still heard screaming. Out of the corner of my eye I saw someone trying to get into the jungle. I aimed from the shoulder and fired. The man dropped, then rose, holding one arm. It was

Sot! I fired round after round at him, but he was already gone. Then suddenly, everything was eerily quiet.

Duane came running to me, carrying a gun and yelling, "The clip, the clip, it keeps falling out!"

"You're pushing the clip release instead of the safety," I yelled at him. His face was snow-white.

"Everything's going wrong!" he screamed. "I got Papsco's carbine but he wasn't in the hut."

Sot had gotten away, and God knows where Papsco and the Old Man were. That meant at least two, maybe three men had gotten away. I had a sudden paranoid vision of one of the guards looking down the sights of his rifle at me. I started running and shouting, "Let's get moving!"

I could hardly believe it when I realized that Nook was still alive and groaning. I aimed at him and pulled the trigger but the gun didn't go off. For a moment I stood there stupidly, and then realized the chamber was empty. I left him and ran around the corner of the fence toward the entrance to the compound, which was our prearranged meeting place in case of a change in plans. Duane came running toward me.

"Where in the hell are the rucksacks?" I yelled.

"In the hut!" he hollered.

"Get them, I'll get the mosquito nets!" I dashed by him to Papsco's hut, only to find it picked clean. Even the shoes that had been hanging underneath the hut were missing. Apparently the Thais had been there before me.

I met Duane with two rucksacks at the entrance to the compound. As I swung one rucksack up on my back, one of the straps broke. The pack was very heavy, far heavier than my own pack. I could barely lift the thing with one hand. "Whose rucksack is this?" I asked Duane, but he shook his head.

Duane began running toward the jungle. He, too, was dragging a rucksack. "Whose is that?" I hollered, but he kept on running, stopping briefly to vomit from the unusual exertion.

Suddenly, a piercing pain in my foot stopped me dead. I had snagged rattan, bristling with fishhook-like thorns. The cuts were deep, baring the white of bone. The pain shot from my foot to my head and I pulled off the rattan and kept running, despite the pain, until I caught up with Duane. We heard the sound of someone coming to our left. Duane and I ducked into the bush and froze. The familiar red head appeared and there were Gene and Y.C., making their way through the jungle. Duane and I jumped up and ran until we caught up with them.

"Hey, Gene, this must be Y.C.'s," I said, dragging the rucksack forward. But Gene was confused, as we all were, and didn't know what I was talking about. Y.C. caught up with us and took the rucksack with a bewildered look. We started to move off together but Y.C. held us back. Then Duane ran on ahead, while I stopped and took hold of Gene's hand.

"Go on, go on," he said. "See you in the States." I looked into Gene's face and got all choked up. I tried to say something but the words wouldn't come. I pumped his hand, began running, then stopped and waved at him and Y.C.

I found Duane all tied up in some thick foliage. "It's no use, it's just too thick," he said. "Let's get out of here!"

We turned and ran back to where we had seen Gene and Y.C. All of a sudden we were at the tiny cornfield we had never seen but about which we had heard the guards talking. The cornstalks towered over us and it was easy running between the rows until we arrived at a huge, natural barrier of thorns. It was about twenty-five feet high and impenetrable. We ran all along the thorn row, looking for a hole, but it was solid as a castle wall. I tried to pry through the heavy thorn bush with my rifle but it was just too thick. Duane stood looking at me and I stared back. On the other side of the ridge lay a reasonable chance of freedom. But the thorns had us cut off. There was nowhere to go.

We were startled by a dog barking close by and turned to find Malay standing beside us. He must have witnessed the whole breakout and then left when we did.

"That dog's going to give us away!" Duane grumbled. He started to move toward Malay to shut him up and instantly Malay turned, ran up a few yards, and disappeared into the supposedly impenetrable thicket. We ran over to where he had vanished and Malay was standing on the other side, whining.

"He's dug a hole right through this thing to go hunting," Duane mumbled behind me as we crawled through the thicket, crossed a slimy creek on the other side, and a few yards beyond that, the base of the ridge. Duane was ecstatic. Somehow I felt that Malay, who was still standing at the fence with his head cocked, had known what was going on.

A few yards up the bank we fell on our knees, folded our hands around each other and closed our eyes in prayer. "God, please help us now. Please let us live!"

Now that we were relatively safe, all my adrenalin seemed to ebb away. When I stood up after praying, I nearly blacked out. The rifle became a heavier burden than I thought possible as it kept digging into my shoulder. The ammunition belt around my waist dragged me down as we moved up on the ridge.

The ground was pocked with hundreds of animal tracks leading toward a puddle on a small shelf. We were both thirsty and I told Duane to cover me as I slowly crawled on my stomach toward the puddle. As I came near, I heard something on the other side. In an instant I was back with Duane in the bush. We both lay there motionless and Duane held his finger across his mouth in a gesture of silence, nodding his head in the direction of the sound. It was quiet there now. I touched Duane lightly, pointing to the M-1 lying out of my reach, and he slid it to me silently. I slipped off the safety and pointed the muzzle toward the noise.

The bush rustled again. There were some whispers but I couldn't see anyone. The bamboo moved and I heard the voices again, only much closer and clearer this time. Duane slid down toward me, his carbine aimed at the sound. Then Procet walked into view. Relief flooded over us but we still didn't dare move, thinking that they, also, were on guard and the slightest noise might draw a bullet from them.

Duane kept his head pressed close to the ground while he waved his hand in the air. Procet saw him and waved back. The puddle was too exposed to be a safe meeting place so we joined the Thais about fifty feet above it.

It was not exactly a meeting of friends, as there had been

plenty of hatred between us in the past, and both groups were now armed. We eyed each other suspiciously, alert for any false move. Procet kept looking at my belt. "How about some ammo?" he asked.

"Okay, but give me a machete in trade. You've got three," I said. I wanted to ask them why they had left me all alone back at the camp, but I kept silent, not wanting to risk a shoot-out. However, all on his own Procet offered an explanation.

"I saw the Old Man and shot him in the leg so he couldn't go for help. But then all the guards ran your way and I couldn't get a single shot off at them. So we got the shoes and let Y.C. and Thani out, and by that time it was all over. Then we left."

They were all wearing shoes and when I asked for mine, Procet said that Y.C. had them. "Oh, yeah, your rucksack," Procet said, holding the bag out to me.

We moved on. Thani cut a way through the foliage with the point of his machete. It seemed stupid to me to make such a trail because trackers could easily follow it, but I didn't say anything. We came across an animal track and followed it, single file, through a long series of switchbacks up the side of the mountain. The trail was a hotbed of leeches, but there was no time to stop and pull them off. Our only hope was to cover as much ground as possible before dark.

The leeches were nothing compared to the worms we came across next. They were everywhere, and it was difficult to walk without stepping on the awful things. Their orange bodies were fat and gleaming with slime and from their backs rose a spiny fin like a dragon's. From their heads grew another horn, similar to a spear. They were as much as a foot long and a half inch thick. Some of them stretched out full length across the trail, while others lay sprawled in various curves. The sight of these creatures turned my stomach more than some of the offal I'd gagged down at Hoi Het. I flicked them out of my path with my rifle.

As we came to the top of the ridge, Thani heard water running somewhere. We were all eager to find it; dehydration had my head spinning. Thani moved ahead and walked down along fallen trees and stopped. We all followed him, hoping to see a valley below, but to our great disappointment the trail wandered downhill for a while and then climbed yet another ridge. We gathered what strength we had and continued walking.

Night had fallen and we were cold, but we kept going. The jungle canopy above us separated from time to time and as I glanced up now and then at the millions of stars above, I wondered if anyone back home sensed that I was now a free man.

The going got steep and rough and we frequently slipped and fell. The ground ripped my bare feet and my clothes snagged constantly on branches and thorns. I didn't know who was in front of me and who was behind. Fatigue had struck us all dumb. What we all needed was water.

We finally came upon a spring, and I stood knee-deep in the ice-cold mountain water and drank thirstily. Every few seconds I lifted my head and looked around like an animal on the alert for predators. As I rubbed my arms I felt the slimy leeches covering them, and I could make out their dark bodies glistening in the faint light of the moon. I noticed that one of my tobacco pouches was missing but I used the other to rub my face and the rest of my body.

We talked very little but agreed on spending the night together. We quietly searched for a place to bed down on this first free night, and then collapsed on an animal trail, with a rock wall to lean on behind us. Duane sat down next to me and it was good to feel the warmth of another human being nearby. I fell asleep quickly.

I awakened with Duane calling my name. I sat up, alarmed. Duane pointed to the sky, the little we could see of it through the heavy foliage. The C-130 was making her evening circles. We looked at each other and lay back down, but I couldn't sleep until the drone of the engines died in the distance.

Something was disturbing my sleep and I awoke to find rain spattering in my face. Duane and I crawled under some huge leaves and held them over our heads to keep off the rain. Soon the drizzle became a downpour and little streams falling off the leaves found their way down our necks. We huddled over our rice, which we knew would mold in a day if it got wet. The downpour turned the dirt into mud so slippery that I slid down the slope for several feet before I could find a root to grab. The noise of the rain in the jungle drowned out every word of panic we yelled at each other. It rained all night. The gray dawn finally brought some relief.

As we slowly made our way down the trail, we noticed that the Thais were wearing plastic rain sheets. "Those damn guys," I muttered. "They were stealing everything they could lay their hands on while I was shooting it out."

"Hey, how about one for us?" Duane asked Procet. Procet shook his head and then Duane asked Phisit, who also refused.

"Then how about enough to cover our rice?" I asked, trying to keep the anger out of my voice. Procet and Phisit talked this over, and Phisit ripped off a piece about a foot square, barely enough to cover the rice in my pack.

The ground was very muddy, making traveling extremely difficult. We clambered up the slope by holding onto vines and roots. At the top we confronted each other to say goodbye, and I saw exhaustion and fear in their eyes as we quietly shook hands. Then Duane and I took a right, and the jungle swallowed us up in a matter of seconds. We never saw the Thais again.

That was the morning of June 30, 1966—the first morning I had seen as a free man in over five months.

11 JUNGLE NIGHTMARE

Thick, heavy fog enveloped us and the ice-cold mist condensed on the jungle vegetation, dripping on us constantly. Leeches and worms were everywhere. There was no possible way anyone could find us on the ridge, as the rain had washed away every trace. Duane and I alternated the lead to keep our pace steady.

The fog became less dense as we got lower. About midmorning we arrived at a muddy stream and forded it, heading toward a thick grassy area. The grass and thorns became thicker and thicker until finally we were trapped and literally couldn't see our hands in front of our faces. We decided to turn around, but the thick grass made it impossible to see which way we'd come. The tall vines and grasses were coated with water droplets and every move brought a cold shower down on us. Millions of mosquitoes whirred about and there were leeches everywhere.

It took us an hour to get back to the muddy stream. We sat down on the bank, exhausted and despondent. The hard reality of the jungle had taken some of the shine off our dream of escape. Prison was bad but at least there had been a pile of leaves to sleep on and a roof to keep off the rain.

We began to travel parallel to the stream and even though this route put us in an exposed position, we thought that we were deep enough into the jungle to be reasonably safe. It began to rain again, and we took cover under some large banana leaves. We sat there, back to back, watching the rain stream from our homemade umbrella. All this exercise after so many months of enforced idleness left us constantly nauseated, but we forced ourselves to check our rice. The small piece of plastic had kept my rice relatively dry but the rain had gotten into Duane's rucksack, swelling his rice into a gooey mess. We ate two handfuls of the soggy rice, then resumed our walk.

We continued to follow the stream in the hope that it would take us to a river where we could build a raft and float our way out. We left the bank, covered with thorns, and started to walk in the water. The muddy water hid the bottom and we stubbed our tender feet until they were swollen and raw.

Finally Duane called out to me, "Dieter, I can't keep going. Let's stop for the night."

"How about one more hour, just one more hour, Duane?"

"Yeah, okay, one more hour," he answered, gulping air like a distance runner. His face was white and his reddish beard contrasted with his auburn hair. His eyes were always big and round, questioning each stop, each hesitation. His green flight suit was matted against his thin, bent-over frame. He looked terrible. I looked away, knowing that I was looking at myself as well as Duane, and the sight frightened me.

We traveled for what seemed like another hour without seeing one sign of civilization and I knew we were already in the impenetrable jungle the villagers had described. Somehow we fought off fatigue long enough to build a crude lean-to, then crawled into it to spend another miserable—but free—night. The rain pounded on us all night, tearing our shelter apart and drenching and chilling us to the bone.

In the morning we knocked down what remained of the shelter to eliminate any trace of our whereabouts, ate a little rice, then moved on downstream. The creek had cleared a bit overnight and we could see some of the rocks at the bottom. Traveling was easier in the clearer water but my bare feet were beginning to show the effects of being wet constantly. The skin was soft and white and was easily punctured by rocks and sticks. Every time I hit something in the water, pain shot up my leg.

We walked all day in the creek, leaving the water periodically to rest and to listen for anyone following us. The creek wound its way into heavy karst terrain, with its bare gray cliffs rising precariously into the sky. An occasional tree emerged wistfully from the craggy walls. The stream became wider in some places and we had to be careful with the current.

In a small clearing where the sun shone brightly through the jungle canopy we checked our direction by pushing a small stick into the ground and putting a pebble at the end of the shadow cast by the stick. After five minutes, we put another pebble at the end of the slowly shifting shadow and repeated this procedure a few more times until we had a true east-west line. We thought we had been going south but found we were traveling in an easterly direction—exactly what we didn't want.

Our rice supply was rapidly dwindling, forcing us to search for other sources of food. We went after a turtle, but weakness made our movements seem as if they were in slow motion, and the turtle easily got away from us. Sadly, we sat down on some rocks by the creek. I picked up a tiny black snail from a colony on the wet rocks. They seemed nearly impregnable in their shells but we found a way to get at them. We found that if the back end of the shell was bitten off, the snail tried to hightail it out the front end. By sucking on the front end and grabbing the thin plate on the bottom of the snail's body, we could pull it out of the shell. We spat out the hard, gristly plate and swallowed the rest of the snail. It was the closest thing to meat we'd had in weeks.

Totally exhausted and needing a good night's rest, we slowly and carefully built a strong lean-to by tying a few bamboo poles to a tree and thatching them with banana leaves. We carpeted the ground with banana leaves and lay down on them, huddling together as the rain again began thundering down from the sky.

We both slept well. In the morning Duane took a handful of rice from his rucksack and shared it with me. It was soggy and green but tasted delicious. Because of the rain we wanted to stay inside where it was relatively dry and warm, but finally had no choice except to get going.

We continued along the stream until we came upon an enormous waterfall dropping into a lagoon thirty feet below. It was a beautiful sight, the mist rising high above the churning white water of the pool below, which was surrounded by lush jungle and wild orchids. Over the roar of the waterfall I tried to tell Duane I would go down first, and ended up motioning to him because the noise was so loud. The going was slippery and wet and the climb down was steep. Suddenly Duane yelled, and I looked up to see him sliding toward me. For a second he regained his footing but then began to tumble head over heels. He knocked me down, and together we cartwheeled into the pool of foaming water.

A lesson I had learned as a boy in Germany many years earlier flashed through my mind. I had fallen into a waterfall and the suction in the pool had held me under. A friend dived in and dragged me out, unconscious. He told me later that the trick was not to surface immediately but to swim away from the suction. I remembered that lesson now as I hit the water. I stayed under as the turbulence of the subsurface waters thrashed about me, and I began swimming away from the falls. I didn't go far but my lungs were nearly bursting when I surfaced. Duane was already out of the water, lying on his back against the smooth rocks surrounding the pool. I floated over to him and crawled out. We lay still for a few minutes catching our breaths, then broke out in hysterical laughter as we inched across and down the slippery boulders to a calm pool.

A creek entered the pool from what we thought to be the west and we decided to follow it. After several hundred yards we came to a waterfall higher than the last one. We started to climb around and over it but halfway up I stopped. The M-1 had banged me for the last time. I yelled down to Duane, "Damn it, Duane, I've just got to get rid of this fuckin' thing!"

He looked wide-eyed and perplexed.

"You've still got your carbine and we can alternate carrying it, but so far we haven't used either one of them." The guns were good only for self-defense, when our backs were really up against the wall. We couldn't use them for hunting, much as we needed meat, because even one shot could bring the Pathet Lao in our direction.

"Yeah, okay," he said, nodding his head.

I wanted to make sure the Laotians couldn't use the gun, so I unloaded it and tried to break the stock off against the rocks. It didn't even crack and pain shot up my arms at each impact. We put the barrel between two rocks and Duane and I laid our weight against it but it still didn't bend. Finally, in total frustration, I flung the gun and the cartridges into the foaming pool beneath the falls.

We didn't get much farther that day. Too tired to build a good shelter, and too exhausted even to eat, we tied a few leaves together and collapsed. The night was freezing cold and we huddled together, arms tightly around each other, as another siege of pouring rain hit us.

In the morning we helped each other to our feet and weakly ate some rice. The rain didn't stop and we half walked, half crawled, muddy and shaking from the cold. The slippery, rocky gully finally came to an end, and water gushed down between two hills on either side of us. I felt as if we were climbing Mount Everest, but in three hours we'd only climbed three hundred feet or so. Our travel brought us to a steep incline, covered by thousands of years of jungle growth, latticed with vines. It was impenetrable but we tried anyway, out of desperation and the thought of a valley beyond.

By midafternoon we had to turn around and retrace our steps. In almost no time we slid down to the place where we had spent the night. We sat there, silently. I turned my head away and began to cry. It was the first time I had cried since our escape, and I let flow out all the fears, anxieties, and frustrations.

The morning did not welcome us, nor did we welcome it. We followed the stream back down toward the waterfall. The dullness of the trip was broken when a wandering bear happened upon us as we were resting. He was large and black, with incredibly fuzzy ears, and across his chest was a splash of white, resembling a crescent-shaped moon. He just stood and looked at us, then lumbered off into the jungle with no apparent fear. We gave him enough time to get well away and then went on downstream. In a very short time we were back at the stream we had chosen in the first place.

We walked dully, without paying too much attention to where we were going. Suddenly, I saw three snakes, bamboo vipers, hanging from a bamboo cluster right in front of Duane's face, coiled and ready to strike. I yelled at Duane to duck, which he did, just missing the hanging snakes. Usually snakes didn't offer us much of a threat, as we moved so slowly that they had plenty of time to hear us coming and slither away to safety.

After the waterfall, the stream gradually grew until it was the size of a little river. When it made a dog-leg turn to the right, we eased ourselves into the water and swam across. We crawled up the ledge on the opposite bank to take a look at the next stretch of water. We couldn't believe our eyes when we saw that the small river widened to about three hundred feet across. Now we could actually begin thinking about building a raft and floating downstream to the Big Muddy.

Our depression lifted and we decided to build a good shelter for the night. It was a very good lean-to, and we even put sides on it. When we crawled into our little house, we had the good feeling that no matter how hard it might rain, we'd be safe and warm inside. That night the wind blew and the rain relentlessly pounded on our door but our sleep was sound and deep and, for the first time, warm.

The following morning when we awoke, we were rested and eager for the day, but lingered in the shelter before going outside to face the cold rain. Duane was coming down with an attack of malaria, and I had a bad cough. My lungs hurt with every breath. I took my two white tablets Gene had given me, but they didn't help. We knelt down and said a prayer, ate some rice, then took apart our beautiful shelter, carefully hiding the parts in the bush.

Because of our weakness, we had no choice but to build a raft from banana trees, which would be easier to build. We worked for hours. I cut down the trees and moved them down to the water's edge, while Duane interlocked them by driving thin bamboo poles through the soft, fleshy trunks. When the raft was finished, we stood waist-deep in the swampy water trying to pull it into the mainstream of the river. It didn't move. In the meantime, several water snakes slipped by and Duane sliced one in half with a swing of the machete. We fervently searched for it, hoping for a meal, but the two pieces had sunk, and we gave up.

We tried again to push and pull the raft into the water but it was a losing battle because it was just too heavy. It had to be lightened, so we cut the raft down to only six trunks. It only supported one man but at least it was light enough to push into the current. Duane took a seat on the raft, while I held on and scissor-kicked behind it to keep it straight in the current. The water was calm and we were just around the bend, about three hundred yards from where we had put the raft in, when Duane jumped off, yelling, "Waterfall!"

How we missed hearing its thunder before we pushed off, I'll never know, but right then wasn't the time to think about it. I swam with all the strength I had and was saved from being swept away only by grabbing hold of some vines trailing in the water.

"Duane, Duane!" I called over the roar.

"Over here!" he called back. He was a little downstream from me, hidden under some overhanging brush. I released my hold on the vines and let the current carry me to him. After many unsuccessful attempts at getting out of the water, we finally found a sturdy root for a handhold and crawled to safety.

What little remained of the day was a waste. We traveled for only another hour, then sat down to eat a cupful of our rapidly dwindling rice. We were too exhausted to build a shelter, so we lay down on a rocky shelf next to the river, hugging each other for warmth, and fell asleep.

In the morning we continued our journey through the thick forest of vines, winding creeks, and steep cliffs to a place where the stream divided. We slid into the calm, clear water, holding onto partly submerged rocks for safety, then floated free and swam feebly to a long sandbar sticking up in the center of the stream. I was in the lead when I saw something move, and froze in place. There, about five feet in front of me, was a ferocious-looking iguana. From his head to his tail was a span of at least four feet. His head was raised and water was dripping from his jaws.

"Sshhh, Duane, look," I whispered to him. Duane didn't say

a word, just let out a deep sigh that meant he was thinking the same thing I was—food. He cautiously handed me the machete and I moved forward ever so slowly, the beast staring at me, unflinchingly. When I was within two feet of him, I raised the machete and swung with every ounce of strength I could muster. The blow instantly killed the lizard. We just stood there, dumbfounded. Duane was smiling the biggest grin I'd ever seen on his whiskered face. We immediately ripped into the iguana and ate our fill of the snow-white flesh, spitting out the skin as we chewed. We could feel strength flow into our bodies as soon as the meat was in our stomachs. We packed away the uneaten portion of the carcass and continued along the peninsula.

We came to a fig tree after only a few hundred feet—it was a doubly lucky day. Most of the figs were rotten and full of worms but we ate them anyway and saved some of them. Between the figs and the meat, we felt healthy and strong, ready and even eager to travel.

The two halves of the stream rejoined, and what we thought was a peninsula turned out to be an island. We crossed the water and continued down the valley where our path led us to a leech-infested area. The ground was covered with their wriggling forms, and just a few feet of walking turned our legs black and red with bloodsuckers. We tried to scrape them off with the machete but it was a losing battle. In the time it took us to get rid of just a few of them, twice that many new ones took hold. It was frustrating and, like two kids being chased by a swarm of yellowjackets, we took off, running as fast as we could.

We came around a bend at a dead run and ran smack-dab into the middle of a rundown guerrilla camp. Duane crashed into me from behind and together we dove into the bush, with all thought of leeches wiped from our minds. Very slowly we crawled closer on our bellies and took a better look. We kept a careful watch for some time before we decided the area was safe. The roofs of the wall-less huts were half rotted away, and apparently the camp had not been used for a long time.

Crouching down, we scurried to the closest frame and climbed into it. We sat there quietly, still not believing our good fortune. Not only had we found food, but we could spend the night off the ground with a roof overhead, and not worry about disassembling and hiding the shelter in the morning. We ate some of the iguana, which had already begun to stink, and some figs. Then we knelt down and said a prayer to beg for no rain for the following day.

When I woke up I was shocked to see Duane all red, from top to bottom. At first I thought something had happened to him during the night. But when we both looked closer, we found hundreds of leeches still attached to him under his clothes and in his hair. They were stuffed so full we could squeeze quantities of blood from them. Duane attended to my back, which he said looked like raw hamburger. One of the leeches tried to go up my rectum but Duane used a couple of sticks like a pair of tweezers and worked it out.

The leeches were a constant hazard and a drain on our strength, but since we had lost our tobacco pouches a long time ago, there didn't seem to be any way to avoid them. The jungle was generally too thick for traveling, and the constant rains made the streams so clouded with mud that we couldn't see the bottom. We were forced to travel on the leech-infested banks of the streams.

We walked until we came to a large pool full of fish, a little farther downstream. We scrounged around for large rocks to throw at them but couldn't find any. We racked our brains to find some other way of getting at the fish but couldn't think of one. However, it seemed like a good place to rest so we took off our clothes to dry in the sun. It was so quiet and peaceful that we both fell sound asleep.

The sensation that my body was on fire woke me. Duane's skin was crimson and his scalp was burned pink under his light hair. I shook him awake, we grabbed our clothes, and moved into the shade to dress.

After a half mile of walking, an attack of nausea and vomiting brought me to a stop. Duane thought the sickness had been brought on by the sunburn but I thought it was probably the worms in the rotten figs. We both had noticed deterioration in our vision; things seemed blurry and unclear. Apparently this was due to hunger because right after we had eaten the iguana, my vision sharpened markedly. However, my eyes were blurring again and I was afraid the damage might become permanent.

As we walked, we decided to throw away the carbine since we just didn't have the strength to carry it. The rucksacks, too, often seemed more trouble than they were worth.

We came to a sandbar several hundred yards beyond the pool, turned around, and walked backwards across the sandbar, hoping to dupe any trackers into thinking we had gone upstream instead of down.

The bush had become very thick again, so we found it easier to crawl. I was three hundred yards ahead of Duane when the smell of smoke stopped me. I waited for him to catch up.

"Do you smell anything?" I asked him.

"No, but look over there." He pointed across the river to where a rice field ran up the slope. About three hundred yards beyond that was a roof barely visible above the grass. We automatically slid into the heavy underbrush next to the river and hid among some fallen logs. We silently ate some rice and the last of the stinking iguana. Within a short time we were fast asleep.

In the night we were awakened by the crashing noise and drenching cold of a heavy monsoon rain. The ground began to give way under us and we started sliding away from the logs. We felt water all around us and knew the rain had swollen the river to such an extent that it had spilled over its banks. The current began to carry us downstream as Duane and I clasped each other for safety. We couldn't see a thing in the pitch-dark. Guided by feel alone, we paddled desperately until we hit the trunk of a tree that had fallen over into the water, its roots still sunk in the bank. We wrapped our legs around it and moved up the tree, water-borne debris tearing at us.

In the first light of dawn, we saw the roofs of three huts only a few hundred feet away. We plunged into the water for cover and pulled ourselves along the trunk of the tree to shore. We weren't alone, however. The bear we had seen near the waterfall was standing on the bank, watching us inquisitively. I swung the machete in his direction, hoping to frighten him away. He acted surprised and calmly sought the cover of a nearby thicket. We waited a few minutes to make sure he wasn't hiding in ambush, then slipped into the jungle toward the roofs.

Duane stayed behind as I crawled closer to observe the village. After a few hours of watching, I was certain the village was abandoned and went back for Duane, who had fallen asleep. We crawled together through the wet leaves to the place where I had been watching, and waited again, just to be safe. Then we quickly crawled into a hut and scanned the area. No sign of life. After a while, we climbed out of the hut and crawled around the other huts to check for tracks on any of the several trails leading to and from the village. The rain had stopped a few hours earlier and had washed away all the old tracks. Any prints in the fresh mud would have indicated that someone had been around very recently, but, fortunately, there were none.

I noticed that Duane wasn't paying much attention to what we were doing and was fighting just to keep from passing out. We went back to the first hut to rest. Duane seemed to grow sicker and sicker. His fever seemed very high, his eyes were sunk deep into their sockets, and he looked as though he was very near death.

"Dieter," he quietly called out to me. His breath was coming in short gasps. "I'm going to die, I know it. Promise me you'll see that Dorcas is all right."

"Sure, buddy, but you're not going to die," I whispered to him. "Hell, I'm sick, too, but we'll both be okay. We'll be picked up soon as we get a fire going, that's for sure. Then they'll take care of us." But even as I said it, listening to Duane's labored breathing, I knew it couldn't come true.

We heard airplanes during the evening, and I thought that a fire might attract a pilot's attention. I split a two-foot-long bamboo tube in half and laid one half on its side on the ground, supporting it with six sticks stuck into the ground. I cut a cross-notch in the center of the other half, scraped some threadlike fibers from the brittle skin of the bamboo, then held them to the inside of the bamboo half, against the notch. I began rubbing the notch back and forth against the razor-sharp edge of the bamboo on the ground, increasing the speed to try to get the fibers smoldering and then blowing to start a flame. Then I would use the flame to set fire to a pile of shredded tinder. We had made a fire in prison this way, but there had been several of us rubbing and blowing. Now, however, I was all alone and too weak to keep rubbing. Duane crawled over to give me a hand but he was even weaker. We had to give up the idea.

In the morning, we left the abandoned village and went back downriver on a small trail. A half mile of traveling brought us to a bamboo raft with a pointed bow and stern similar to that of a canoe. Duane and I each knew what the other was thinking: our walking was finally at an end. Tonight we would float to freedom. It must have been about eight in the morning, so we went a little deeper into the jungle to wait out the day some thirty feet from the raft. The rest was needed and welcome, but we had to deal with a new pest—flies so tiny they could be seen only when the sun glinted off their wings. Despite their size, they packed a bite twice as bad as that of a mosquito. For protection, I covered my legs with wet leaves, pulled the rucksack over my head, and stuck my hands underneath my body. But the little pests still found their way to my flesh. In spite of the constant torment, the rest did both of us good, particularly Duane.

When it was just about completely dark, we slid down to the the canoe-raft, untied the rattan that secured it to a tree stump, and climbed in. I whispered to Duane to hold onto the machete to keep from losing it through the cracks between the bamboo poles. We were sitting in three inches of water on the bottom of the raft, while the river's current carried us away. The moving water floated us into some brush and we had a difficult time pushing away. We heard voices along the shore and knew we were passing a village. We silently floated by two more villages and then heard the nearby roar of rapids. Around midnight the moon rose and flooded the water with silver light. Large rocks loomed ahead, and with the long bamboo pole I had found in the raft, I pushed us away from them. The river narrowed and its pace quickened, spilling us into a wide, slow-moving body of water.

Suddenly we heard a tremendous thundering noise just ahead of us. Before we had time to react, our canoe shot out over a waterfall toward the churning waters of the pool at the base of the falls. I was in the bow and the nose dive tumbled Duane into me like a rolling stone. The canoe plunged into the water, then shot out again, bouncing like a cork. The rapids took hold of the partially broken canoe. We hung onto what remained, our eyes glued to the foaming waters in front of us. Then, with as little warning as the waterfall had given us, the water was calm once more. I glanced behind and saw Duane hanging onto the other end of the poles. He stuttered that the machete was gone, but he seemed unhurt.

A villager was standing knee-deep in the water, fishing. Just as we saw him, he saw us. He called out, but we couldn't understand him. He yelled again, but we remained silent, like two ghosts, and floated past him in the dark. He jumped up and ran for the shore in the shallow water. We scrambled to the bank, abandoning the remains of the canoe.

The night was almost over as we dragged ourselves along the shore and suddenly came upon a sleeping village. On our right was the dark silhouette of a hut, but we went right past it. No one saw or heard us, not even the dog lying next to the hut. We edged back toward the river and heard the sounds of voices on the opposite bank and saw lit cabangs. We wondered if it was a search party looking for us.

Dawn was on us before we knew it. In the last fading minutes of the night, we crossed the river to look for a hiding place in the deep jungle on the other side. Thousands of insects surrounded us, but we soon fell asleep in spite of them.

Hours later we awoke to find that the tiny flies had feasted on our faces, turning them as swollen and red as our feet. In terrible pain, we covered ourselves with rotten leaves and spent another six miserable hours under the steaming leaves in the hot sun.

During the afternoon Duane and I discussed our plans. Now that we had been spotted, floating down the river was too dangerous. We decided, instead, to cross a ridge, hoping to find another river. We had the mad idea that we could float out to the *Ranger*. Our chances of making it, of course, even if we had been in good physical shape, were easily several million to one, but we adopted the crazy scheme out of desperation. Only the impossible seemed possible at that point.

We took off in the late afternoon, carefully making our way through a rice field. It was easy traveling, as all the undergrowth had been cleared away. Mosquitoes of a different type—covered with white dots and having hind legs an inch long—began to swarm around our heads so thickly they obstructed our vision. Oddly enough, they never attacked us, just continued their nerve-racking hum.

The cleared field came to an end but we still made good time up the gentle slope. During the climb, we stopped and looked back at the magnificent view: the trees, flowers, and a cloud of mist hanging over the waterfall that made everything shine with an incandescent light. Exquisite blue butterflies sometimes settled next to us with no apparent fear and, for a few seconds, helped us forget the ugliness and futility of this impossible struggle. From the top of the mountain we could see the countryside for miles. The land was an endless succession of ridges. About fifteen miles away, a huge ridge, taller than the rest, rose above the purple haze.

"The divide between Laos and Vietnam!" Duane exclaimed. "If we can get across it, we'll be able to see the ocean and soon be home free." I was awed by the sight. The fact that we could see our goal started us walking at a quicker pace. Way up to our left were a couple of huts nestled in the rice fields. I remembered Procet telling us that during the rice-planting season the Laotians lived on the fields, and when the planting was finished, they abandoned the huts and returned to their villages. I thought that if only we had something we could use to signal an airplane, the empty rice field would be a perfect place to do it.

"A chopper wouldn't have any trouble landing here," Duane answered my unspoken thoughts. His eyes had a faraway look.

As we traveled down the other side of the ridge, we went back into such dense jungle that even the mosquitoes couldn't follow us. When I stumbled, the underbrush was so thick that instead of landing on the ground and tumbling downhill, I hung suspended on the foliage in front of me. As suddenly as the jungle had swallowed us up, it spat us out into a little clearing. In the forest beyond, tall trees, straight as sentinels, towered over the wet brown ground. The odor of decaying leaves and new growth reminded me of the Black Forest in Germany. A wave of nostalgia swept over me.

We hurried down the remaining slope to find at the bottom a tiny spring which, as usual, was covered with leeches. We scraped them away with a stick, then lay on our bellies to drink our fill. The little spring of water soon blossomed into a creek that in turn, only minutes later, joined a wide river new to us.

It was too good to be true—not only a new river but two rafts, one on either side of the river. This river probably went to the ocean.

Now we had to be extra careful, since rafts meant people. As we walked down an animal trail, we found snakes and turtles and even heard some frogs, but were too slow to catch any of them. The river then bent its way around to the right. We decided to hide and wait until dark. As soon as we left the trail a villager and his woman passed not more than thirty feet away from us. We sat silently, aware of how close we'd come to being seen. Luck had been with us but for how long? Our caution even led us to abandon the idea of stealing a raft to float downstream. The incident with the fisherman had been much too close. We were fairly sure there was a village nearby and to chance floating past it was surely to court danger. When darkness fell we went upriver and crossed to the opposite bank.

The stars came out and we knew there would be no rain. I wrapped some of my torn clothes around my legs and went to sleep.

Early the following morning we began traveling again along the river. We were more dead than alive. I had been vomiting blood and my lungs ached terribly. I was afraid I had tuberculosis. I knew if we didn't get out of the jungle soon, we'd both die.

In the midst of these despairing thoughts, I suddenly heard a child's voice. As if on command, Duane and I instantly jumped out of the trail and hid in the brush. Peeking out we saw a small boy playing with a dog, only a few hundred yards from us. To evade him, we sneaked up the side toward the ridge next to us and found ourselves in the middle of a field of corn. I turned around to Duane and pointed eagerly to the small green cobs all around us. We began eating some and stuffing more into our rucksacks. Duane seemed to be making too much noise and I nudged him with my foot to quiet him. Then we heard the voices of a man and a woman.

I was worried, since we had stolen a lot of the corn and it would be an obvious sign of our presence. As silently as possible we inched our way through the field closer toward the ridge, when I sensed someone coming. Not more than a hundred feet away a young boy and girl were walking downhill toward us. I motioned to Duane not to move and whispered in his ear about the two Laotians. He raised his head to look and crouched back, fear written across his face. Blood was pounding in my ears. We talked by gestures, and Duane suggested turning around and going back the way we'd come. I shook my head. The two villagers had stopped and were picking what looked like peppers from a bush.

Keeping them in sight, we slowly crawled between the stalks toward the jungle, stopping dead in our tracks each time they moved. The young people were working their way down the line of bushes they were harvesting. Each time they moved from one bush to the next, we crawled a few feet closer to the jungle.

With a sigh of relief we left the corn and began working our way through a small rice field bordered by heavy jungle. Once, the boy stopped his picking and stared in our direction for what must have been five minutes. We lay motionless until he finally resumed his work, then crept on toward the jungle where we would feel safe again.

The jungle lasted for only fifty yards, however, before giving way to a second rice field and a large clearing. We were afraid to cross the clearing since someone was almost certainly around. Crouched down, we skirted the clearing and made our way up to the top of the ridge. Luck was still with us.

A few feet into the cover of the jungle, we sat down to rest. A good breeze was blowing to keep the mosquitoes away. We ate some more of the corn, and after we finished, I had my first bowel movement in over a week. We considered camping on top of the ridge for a few days to steal more corn but decided it was too dangerous to stay in one place.

Following the edge of the jungle down the other side of the hill, we stumbled across a stream bed with a trickle of running water. We nearly drank it dry, then traveled downhill along the stream bed until the water vanished underground and the bed became only a gully. At the bottom of the gully Duane found some berries that resembled little green olives, and we wondered whether or not it would be safe to eat them. I picked up a berry, held it behind my back, and told Duane to choose a hand. Duane lost, but as soon as he took his first bite, I took one also.

A heavy rustling overhead sent us scurrying for cover. Fortunately, it was only some monkeys leaping around in the trees. They, too, had been picking the green berries, and the fruit we'd gathered from the ground was what the monkeys had dropped.

We went on downhill. The foliage became thicker and heavier. We hadn't gone very far when we came to a crude bamboo fence that ran up the hill to the right of the creek. We followed the fence for about thirty yards, then climbed over it into a small field loaded with red peppers.

"Look, sugar cane!" Duane whispered in my ear, pointing to some tall, purple sticks growing beyond the peppers. We cautiously made our way to the stand of cane and broke off some of the stalks. As I bit into the cane, I felt something crumble in my mouth. It turned out to be one of my front teeth.

I knew the missing tooth made my already miserable appearance doubly bad. "How do I look?" I asked Duane. He didn't say a word, just kept munching on the cane, stuffing more of it into his rucksack and shirt. We gathered up our splendid spoils and slipped back into the cover of the jungle to continue the feast.

I walked a short distance away to relieve myself, but what came out of me was more frightening than relieving. My urine was dark red and my feces were white and laced with little, wiggling worms. The fear must have still been on my face when I returned to Duane.

"What's wrong?" he asked. Rather reluctantly, I told him about my dark urine. Somehow I didn't want him to know. "Yeah, mine's been the same way for the past three days," he said. That made me feel a little less alone but not any less sick.

I decided to explore the area. Duane stayed where he was. I found a narrow trail leading to the creek and then paralleling it into the bush toward the bank of an unseen river. I came across some pepper plants and a few corncobs that had been picked nearly clean. Since these were signs that people could be around, I kept hidden as much as possible. I pushed the covering brush aside and looked across the creek. Several abandoned huts sat in a small clearing along the river. Something about them rang a bell in the back of my memory. I checked each detail against the picture in my mind and, as soon as I was sure, heartsickness and despair overcame me. I knew we had been here before. At first I wanted to hide the truth from Duane, but he would find out on his own soon enough.

"Don't panic," I said as soon as I got back to him, "but get ready to be sick." His eyes searched my face. "You know that abandoned village we spent the night at a few days ago?" He nodded. "Well, it's just across the creek over there."

"I don't believe you!"

I led him to the spot from where we could see the huts, and the two of us crouched there staring at the sight without saying a word. Finally the horror of it grew too awful to handle and the tears flowed. Disoriented by the floating, curved ridges and the twisting river, we had traveled in a circle. All of our suffering had been for nothing. We had crossed a ridge and thought we'd found a new river, when we had actually floated around a mountain by night, climbed over it, and come back to the same river.

We sat there until dark, then crossed the creek and went into the hut where we had spent a night before. In the dark, despair grew even worse. We felt we were at the end of the line. The river—the one that was to float us to Vietnam—in fact merely flowed deeper into Laos. There was no escape. Upriver was the prison camp, downriver were the Pathet Lao looking for us, and to the sides were impenetrable jungles and endless rows of high ridges. We were trapped. The only possible way out was air contact, but the only way to attract an airplane was with fire and smoke, and we were far too weak to make a fire.

Suddenly an idea flashed into my mind. As my spirits lifted I grabbed Duane. I remembered that when we had been following the river downstream a few days earlier, Duane had given up on carrying the carbine and thrown it into the river. "Duane, the ammo, the ammo!" His look was one of amazement, as if he didn't know what I was talking about. "Remember when you dumped the carbine in the river? Well, I threw the ammo in after it. If I could find them again, we could use the powder to build a fire!" Duane was barely able to nod his agreement to the idea when fatigue won and he fell fast asleep. I followed.

The chill of the morning and Duane's shaking awakened me. He was having an attack of malaria and asked me to cover him, but there was nothing to use. I lay as close to him as possible to give him some of my body's warmth but it didn't even begin to help. He continued to shake violently. He was obviously too sick to come with me to look for the discarded cartridges, but I couldn't just leave him in the hut with the possibility of some villager wandering through and finding him. I dragged him into the bush and covered him with wet leaves, leaving only his head bare. He lay as still as a corpse. I shook his hand and left.

As a warning device, I laid a piece of rattan across each of the trails leading into the camp. Anyone coming in would knock the piece out of place. I planned to check all the strings when I returned. Then I started upriver.

I slid into the cold water and was swept downriver for about a hundred feet until I smashed against a large rock. I cut across there to the other side and climbed out.

Travel along this side went much more easily than I had expected and, fortunately, I also remembered the place where we had thrown the carbine into the water. The river had risen, then receded, hiding everything with a thin coat of mud. I remembered that when Duane had thrown the carbine away he'd said that nobody, not even he, could ever find it again. After searching for a while, I was sure Duane had been right, and concentrated on finding the cartridges rather than the gun.

"Please, God, let me find it," I kept repeating. My fingers were searching under the mud when I saw the tail end of a carbine round. I jumped on it and fell on my knees, kissing the cartridge and saying a prayer of thanks. I was ecstatically happy and wanted to get back and share the happiness with Duane. Searching until it was too dark to see, I found three more. I wedged the slugs into a crack in a rock and worked the casings back and forth until the lead pulled free of the cartridge neck. Then I carefully transferred the powder from the cartridge into a small bottle that Crazy Horse had discarded after giving himself the vitamin shots in the camp.

I awoke in the middle of the night aware of something moving in the bush. I sat up, completely alert. Whatever it was, it wasn't more than a few feet away and was moving very quietly. I could feel its presence coming closer in the dark and my head was pounding, but I didn't move a hair. Then the thing was breathing on me with a warm, foul-smelling breath, and I knew it was the bear. His face was only inches from mine when I let out a loud and chilling scream, jumping up. He let out his own growl as we fell over each other and I scrambled to get away. Then, suddenly, silence. I sat there, listening for the bear, but everything was quiet. I felt in my pocket and the bottle was safe and unbroken.

At dawn I began retracing my steps, occasionally crossing huge bear prints. I bypassed any obstacles I came across by easing into the water and letting the current take me around them, carrying the bottle in my mouth to keep it dry. Fording the river again was surprisingly easy. When I neared the place where I had left Duane, I checked the rattan strings across the trails and found there had been no intruders.

Duane was lying just as I had left him. I ran to him and cradled him in my arms. Then I felt his arms clasp me and knew he was still alive. We hugged each other and cried because we were so relieved to be together again. I showed Duane the bottle and his face lit up at the sight of the beautiful, black powder. Despite his weakness he held the bottle before his eyes, tears rolling down his face, and kept saying, "That's great!"

I went back underneath the hut to gather up the dry bamboo I had tried to light the first time we'd been here. Duane crawled over to join me and we attempted to set off a little powder six times with no success. We'd gotten little spurts of flame going, but not long enough to ignite the bamboo. We had only enough powder left for one last try.

"Wait," Duane said, as I was preparing to use the last of the powder. "We definitely need some charcoal." We found a few pieces lying around the hut, and I again stuffed the notch in the bamboo with shavings and powder, attempting another fire. When it caught, I picked up the tiny flame in the palm of my hand and nursed it with fine bamboo filings. The pain was intense but I didn't dare drop the bit of tinder. Duane laid a piece of charcoal next to the flame and blew on it. The red pinhead of a glowing ember appeared on the stick. I dropped the fire in my hand and together Duane and I blew on the red coal as I held another piece of charcoal against Duane's piece. We kept blowing until we had a piece of glowing charcoal the size of a walnut.

We kept a small fire going until dark, then let it get a little larger. During the day I had made some torches by tying dry leaves from the hut to the end of bamboo poles, and we sat with our fire and flares, waiting for the first sound of an aircraft engine. As we sat there waiting and hoping, I decided to take advantage of the time and the fire to cook us a hot meal, our first in over a month. I'd found a bamboo container in one of the huts and stuffed it with some tapioca leaves, bark, a bit of rice, and a piece of sugar cane, adding a little water at the last. I stuck the container into the fire, as was the local custom. It sprang a leak, very nearly drowning our small fire. The hot, crude stew was delicious.

Duane and I heard the hum of the airplane's engines at the same time and jumped up, sending our food flying. We lit our torches and ran out of the hut into the night. It was already too late and the plane had passed over and gone beyond us. Our disappointment eased, however, as we looked up into the sky and saw it was a perfect night for signaling aircraft. We knew we'd have more opportunities. Two more planes flew over, and each time we lit the torches and ran out but we were always too slow. The problem was fatigue, and as the night wore on it was difficult just to stay awake. We woke each other to alternate with fifteen-minute watches but we still fell asleep before the time was up. We dumped cold water on ourselves, but nothing worked. We were just too close to the end of our rope.

We were both asleep when the sound of engines again awakened us. The fire was burned down very nearly to nothing, just enough to light the torches. The sound of the engines didn't fade away into the distance this time, and we heard the pilot give power as he made a turn. Duane was wildly waving his torch in an "S" and I was waving mine in an "O." Duane began yelling that the plane had seen us and I yelled at him to shut up, but he just kept on yelling. Making a fire had been a big enough risk but Duane's yelling was sure to bring the Pathet Lao down on us. Finally I had to jump on him to shut him up.

"Dieter, I'm sorry, but he sees us, he sees us! We'll be safe! Oh, God, he sees us!" The C-130 turned around and came back in our direction. "Hey, they're going to take a bearing and distance reading on this place!" Duane said.

The first flare dropped from the plane and it lit up the sky brilliantly. We stood there, unable to move, trying to get hold of the thought that we would soon be safe. A second flare fell. Now we knew it was no dream—we had been noticed and would be picked up the following morning. The flares drifted over the ridge to our right and their light disappeared. Duane and I hugged each other and cried for joy as we watched the C-130 leave. All we had to do now was stay alive until morning and welcome the chopper. After all we'd been through, it almost seemed too easy.

We hurried back to the fire and sat, too numb with hope to talk. After thinking about it for a while, we decided to wait out the time in the brush, as Duane's shouting and the sight of our torches might easily have attracted some unwanted attention. We moved out to the place where I'd laid the mat for Duane to sleep, and every hour or so one of us would go back and stoke the tiny fire. We didn't want to take a chance on losing it in case something should foul up.

As we sat in the brush, we seemed to be safe already. It was almost as if we were back home again.

"We finally made it," Duane said with that faraway look in his eyes.

"In less than four hours we'll be in the chopper!" I said.

"Listen, you're going up on the hoist first!" he exclaimed. "I know how they work and I'll help you. Boy, I'm going to have scrambled eggs and ham for breakfast!" As he said this my mouth began to water. "There's always food on the chopper," Duane assured me. "So we can have something to eat right away!"

"Where do you think they'll take us first?" I asked him. "Will my buddies ever be surprised to see me! They'll probably say, "Hey, you ol' Kraut, so you made it. Bet they had a hard time with you!"

"After I eat breakfast, I'm going to call Dorcas, just like that."

It began to drizzle and before we knew it, we were soaking wet. "What if it's too cloudy and overcast for the chopper to come in?" I had awful visions of our helicopter forced to return to base because of the weather.

"You're kidding?" Duane said. "A chopper can fly in anything, man, anything."

Every now and then Duane would break the silence and say, "Don't worry, this drizzle won't stop them—they'll come, hell or high water."

With the dawn, our excitement began to peak. Anytime now the chopper would come in for us. Duane and I sat silently, waiting for the first sounds of rotors cutting the thick morning air. The sky grew lighter and the minutes ticked by. Soon it was full day, with no sign of the chopper.

"Let's give them time," Duane said. "The ceiling's low. Maybe they're having trouble finding us."

But already I was having pangs of doubt, and with each minute the pangs grew into something more like full-fledged depression. We waited and hoped, but the more time that passed, the more our hope for freedom and home faded away. We were so drained that tears wouldn't even come. We felt betrayed by our own people. Our buddies had left us out here in the vast, God-forsaken jungle while they all sat around, dry and happy in a bar somewhere, probably talking about the crazy villagers who had waved torches at them.

Finally it got to be too much. I screamed, "You idiots, what in the hell's the matter with you? Don't you know we've broken out?"

"I guess the others haven't gotten out, either," Duane said. "Otherwise, they'd be here by now—they would know to be on the lookout for us."

"They just had to know, dammit!" I said aloud.

We were both cussing, blaming God for not helping us. Then, exhausted by anger and despair, we were silent.

The rain was falling gently as if it would never stop. We didn't know what to do, where to go tomorrow. There seemed to be no way out.

12 RESCUE

With the disappointment of the morning, Duane's malaria grew steadily worse. He lay in the brush, hardly breathing or speaking to me. The day passed, and I wondered if we would make it through the night.

As we lay there, Duane suddenly rasped, "Go on, go on, Dieter." His yellow eyes stared straight ahead. "Leave me alone —I don't want you around here anymore. I want to die by myself. Just tell Dorcas everything. I'm going to die right here."

"You're nuts, you're crazy. Nobody's going to die here!" I assured him. But only a little bit earlier I myself had wanted to die. Now I was hoping we might get picked up that night, after all. We couldn't give up.

"I wonder why they didn't come in," Duane mumbled.

"I don't know. Maybe they thought it was a trap. You never know!" We nursed the little fire throughout the day and the evening but it was little use. The weather was too bad for flying. Duane and I gave up waiting and slept until the following morning. It was still windy and raining when we woke.

"Dieter, I'm going down toward the village," Duane announced. "I'm going to go down and steal some food," he added.

"That's a sure way of getting yourself killed, you know that?" I told him.

"I'm not going to get caught. We need food; we can't last." He paused. "If I get caught, maybe they'll be friendly and we can get some medical help." He paused again, then said, "I'm going, Dieter," with an air of finality.

I tried to stop him a couple of times, but it was no use. "Okay, but you're not going alone. We're going together." Maybe he was crazy but I was too sick and starved to care. We piled lots of wood on the fire to keep it going until we returned, then slowly made our way down the trail toward the river. We didn't get very far that morning, stumbling along and holding on to each other for support.

Suddenly Duane stopped. "Animal traps, bunches of them."

We had walked right into the middle of a whole set of traps. It was a miracle we hadn't set one off already. By all rights, both of us should have been hanging head down, dangling by the foot from a snare rope. We had recognized the traps from the little gates the villagers built to guide the animals into them, and by the bent-over trees that would jerk the animal up once the trigger was set off. We didn't dare move an inch. The only way out was to retrace our steps, exactly.

"Duane, pick up that stick next to you and give it to me. I'm going to try to find the triggers and set off as many of them as I can." As I worked, probing the ground, I felt as if I were working in the middle of a mine field, and any second could be my last. Twenty minutes later, I had sprung four traps. The triggers were cleverly hidden and very sensitive—it took only an ounce of weight to set them off. Then a bent tree snapped erect with the sound of a whip cracking, and the empty noose tied to it hung high and quivering above us. It was a chilling sight.

Once we were out, Duane and I sat down to assess our situation. Those traps meant that there were certainly people nearby. But we were so weak and tired that we couldn't think of any kind of plan. The only thing we could do was keep on moving.

We had crawled some more, probably less than a quarter of a mile, when we came to a few huts that had been abandoned so long their roofs were collapsing. Before venturing in, we waited at the outskirts and kept a close watch. We'd found out from experience that it was usually safe to go into an abandoned village at noon because the villagers came to pick their crops at dawn or at dusk. We waited anyway, just to be sure. To our surprise, there was a Jersey cow tied to a pole. I tried to milk her but she was dry. She didn't protest at my poking and pulling, just watched me silently and patiently. I put my arms around her neck and she felt warm and smooth, the first thing I had touched so tenderly in six months. Finally, Duane grew impatient and called me to him, so I left the cow reluctantly.

We looked for food but all we found was some kind of green fruit that tasted so bad we couldn't get it down. Then we spotted a crazy-looking, scraggly cat that took off like a bolt of lightning as soon as we moved toward her.

We pushed on, crawling in the slippery red mud along the river. The trail narrowed to only a couple of feet, making it hard for us to travel side by side. Then the trail turned left, dipping into a twenty-five-foot-deep gully and back out again. It made a sharp right around a cluster of bamboo, and suddenly a little boy carrying water containers was standing a few feet to our left. Duane and I said, *"Sabay,"* which means hello. The boy nodded and walked away, taking no further notice of us.

Seconds later, somebody off to my right yelled, *"Americali,"* and a villager jumped out of the bush a few feet away. With his cry of *"Americali"* the jungle came alive with people, running and screaming. A villager appeared before us, clutching a long machete in both hands, high above his head. I was on my knees to Duane's left and Duane was also kneeling on the ground, holding his prayer-folded hands toward the villager, who still held the machete over his head. I yelled, *"Sabay"* to the man and started to get up. He hesitated for an instant, then slashed at Duane, who had dropped to his haunches. The blade disappeared into Duane's leg, just below the groin. Awful screams burst from Duane as the villager let the machete fall again, burying it deep into Duane's neck. His head fell forward.

Not ten seconds had passed since we had seen the boy. I stood up with my mouth open, stumbling backwards and not comprehending what I was seeing. The blood shot from Duane's neck in long, pulsating leaps, spattering everywhere, and I realized suddenly just what was happening. The villager was swinging the machete at me. I ducked under the blow, thrusting my hands toward him. He then ducked and ran, thinking I was making a move. The next thing I knew, I was running back down the trail toward the gully and then on up the gully, leaving the trail. I had only gone twenty feet into the brush when I saw five villagers with machetes run past on the trail behind me.

Then the reality and horror caught up with me. I was scrambling uphill for my life. Only a moment before, I could barely crawl, much less walk, but now I seemed to be going faster than I had ever gone before. I moved without thinking; my body took over.

Fifteen feet ahead the gully forked and I went up to the right for about fifty feet, leaving deep footprints in the soft mud, then backtracked quickly, setting my feet into the prints I had already made. I jumped to a rock and then stepped from one leaf pile to another and went up the left fork, being very careful not to break a twig or leave any other sign. I was twenty feet up the left fork, just going over a small knoll, when I heard them following my tracks on the right side. Steadily and silently I moved up the steep gully wall. My heart and head were banging loudly and I thought my body was going to explode with the pressure. I could actually feel the blood course throughout my entire body and watched my chest heave with each beat of my heart. I heard the trackers yell as they came to the end of my fake tracks.

Suddenly I was on a narrow trail that ran along the top of the gully. I pulled back and looked both ways, then jumped across it and ran a few feet into the brush before collapsing. Not thirty seconds later, two women and three soldiers hurried by on the trail. They were all armed with rifles and one of the women stopped right in front of me while the others moved on. She faced the other way and seemed to be watching the gully intently. Instantly, I knew what was happening: they were setting up a search perimeter around the area where they thought I was. By sheer chance and God's help, I had slipped through it with a few seconds and ten feet to spare. I couldn't understand why she didn't hear my deep and rapid breathing. Even though I tried to suppress it, it was hopelessly loud.

Moving ever so slowly and keeping the woman in sight, I inched my way on my back deeper into the jungle. One time she heard something and turned around, searching the area. I waited, stock-still, for her to turn around again, then inched away until she was out of sight. The farther I got, the faster I let myself go. At first it was inch by inch, then foot by foot, and now I was moving evenly and steadily. One thought pushed me on—that the fire would still be alive when I got back to the abandoned village. I took a few steps, stopped and listened for the sound of pursuers, then took a few more steps. I heard women's voices way off and then there was yelling closer by, and I realized it was the guards on the search perimeter, confused by the way I'd slipped past them.

At the very top of the ridge I came out onto a wide animal trail and had gone along it for only a short distance when I recognized the country. Duane and I had traveled through there a few days earlier when we had mistakenly gone in a circle. I steadily followed our earlier path down the creek, toward the old abandoned village.

Occasionally I stopped to listen. The villagers' voices were farther and farther away and soon I couldn't hear them at all. When I reached the village, I didn't even bother to check for people. I ran in under the hut, flopped on my stomach, and began searching for a live coal in the remains of the fire. Only after I got to the very bottom did I find a glowing ash, the size of my little fingernail. I nursed the cinder into a roaring fire.

I began to hallucinate and suddenly my fear of death was gone. I didn't care if the villagers found me and actually wanted them to come and shoot me as I was sitting next to my fire. Night came very soon, but I didn't sleep. I decided to put on a real show, to go out with a bang. Making no attempt to hide myself, I ran around the village and collected everything flammable I could find. I tossed it all into a pile next to the fire and waited. Those lousy, fucking pilots had let us down. Maybe they'd thought it was a trap, but I was going to give them a show they wouldn't forget.

During the night I heard the far-off whine of the C-130's engines. I lit a long torch in the fire and held it to the edge of the hut's roof, setting it on fire. I ran to the second hut while the first hut, full of old, dried baskets and mats, burned as fast as tinder. Systematically, I set the whole village on fire, running between the huts, shielding my face from the intense heat. The C-130 flew over and dropped one flare after another until the sky was white. I was yelling, cursing at them, and they kept on dropping flares. The village burned away in almost no time and only the glowing bamboo frames of the huts remained—skeletons in the flare-infested night. I collapsed in the brush near the spot where Duane and I had hidden only the day before, and began sobbing loudly. Deeper and deeper the sobs racked my body. I was crying for Duane, for myself, and for the other guys who had escaped with me.

Rain spattering in my face woke me up. I couldn't shake the feeling that this was all unreal, that life was nonexistent, and everything I did or felt was a dream. Slowly my mind admitted that this nightmare was real, not imagined. I tried to find shelter in an unburned corner of one of the skeletal huts, but soon the wind pushed the wall over. I spent the time until dawn lying in deep mud with the rain streaming over me.

I couldn't believe that a part of me was anxiously awaiting the day. I had nothing to look forward to, but like the glow of a tiny bit of charcoal, a small hope remained that I could still be rescued. I had visions of flares drifting to earth on little parachutes with radios and people dangling from them. Another part of me kept saying that I had seen the flares in a dream, that they weren't real either.

Before dawn came I began hunting for the parachutes even though I didn't believe in them. It was raining so hard I could hardly see, and the only source of light was an occasional bolt of lightning. I hunted like a blind man, until at daybreak I found myself looking at the white of a small parachute snagged in the top of several large bushes, about one hundred feet away from me. Disregarding the thorns tearing at me, I started pushing through the bushes toward the parachute, but couldn't quite get to it. It was like another nightmare when something you want or need is just out of reach and, try as you might, you can't get to it. Then I found myself going around to the other side of the bushes, and from there I could reach up and touch it easily. I took hold of one corner of the parachute and pulled the whole thing down. The parachute felt soft, as if it were made of velvet. I buried my head in it and rubbed my face with its soft, wet folds. This parachute was from home and it reminded me of where I was going. With the parachute in my hands, I no longer doubted that it was real, and now that I had it, my mind again locked into one idea: rescue.

I forded the river where I'd crossed it before, as my mind shifted back and forth from fantasy to reality. Had it been several days? A month? A year? I remember searching for the ammunition and using it to build a fire. I felt very alone and wished Duane were with me, but Duane was too sick to come along. I concentrated every bit of strength on getting up to the hut in the old rice field we had seen a week ago, across from the village that I had burned. I could remember it was a beautiful field and it ran all the way up into the sky. I had to stop because the field was spinning around and around in front of my eyes. I begged Duane to help me, to hold my head up.

It was an eternity before everything fell into place and I realized I had simply become dizzy crawling up the 45-degree slope of the rice field. Three hundred yards up the slope was a strip of level ground. I knew I had to keep going to get to that level ground before the chopper came and before the enemy found me. I began crawling again. "Boy, I'll bet those PLs are scared now. First they saw the village burning, then all those flares. They probably think the whole U.S. Army is coming to wipe them out for killing Duane." I liked that idea. "Damned right they are. The whole damn army; better yet, the marines. Just you wait!"

I kept mumbling as I crawled, thinking grand thoughts of the whole U.S. military coming in and letting all those bastards have it, all the while keeping my eyes on the roof of the abandoned shelter up in the field. That shelter was my final goal. I began talking to the plants around me. "This is the last hill I'm going to climb in this stinking jungle," I told them. Every few seconds I turned around, anxiously expecting to hear the chopper. I had the parachute all ready for signaling. There was no way I was going to be too slow this time—I was going home. "Come on, you guys, what're you waiting for?"

Hours later I made it to the small hut. It had collapsed and the roof was lying on the ground. The jungle had grown up high around it but I was able to slip inside. The high elephant grass pretty well cut off the view to the outside but it was a good place to wait. It was probably about eight o'clock in the morning now, only a short while until the sun would come over the ridge. I could tell it was going to be a clear and beautiful day, a perfect day for rescue. As I lay and waited, I began thinking about Duane again. I tried to shake the image of his naked corpse out of my mind. "No more, please God, no more," I begged, as I scrambled out of the hut. I knelt in the entrance and looked up. A great golden door opened in the sky and from the doorway came a huge crowd of skiers. Some of them could ski very well but the others kept falling down and complaining that their legs were too cold. I blinked my eyes hard. At first I felt as if I were looking at someone else's dream, but then things began to fall into focus—I was staring into the sun.

I crawled around outside and laid out the parachute. I was in a really great place, exposed to planes in the sky but hidden from the enemy below. Time passed, hour by hour, but there was no sound of an approaching plane or chopper, and I sat there, hallucinating in the sun.

I waited all day but not a single plane flew over, not even a jet at 40,000 feet. I wondered if it was a Sunday or a national holiday and if all the pilots were off work. Then I decided that this was the last thing I was going to do in this jungle—I wasn't taking another step. I was just going to lie in the little hut and die of starvation. If a pilot saw my signal, that was fine. If not, that was fine, too. "God, please forgive me for all the bad things I've done in my life. Please be good and let me die soon." I pleaded this way with God over and over until I fell asleep.

I kept waking up, asking myself what those guys in the C-130 were thinking. "Didn't they wonder why a whole damn village was burning down? Didn't they have sense enough to wonder what it was all about? Didn't they report it?" I kept repeating the same questions, but there didn't seem to be any answers. I began to hope for rain as I became more and more painfully thirsty. Much as I tried to imagine things other than water, my mind would think of nothing else.

When night came I fell into a deep sleep. In the morning I was no longer resigned to death. "To hell with this," I told myself out loud. "I'm not going to stay here and die. I'm going to walk right over to Vietnam and then swipe me a sampan and float out to the carrier. Since they aren't coming to me, I'm going to them!"

I stuffed the parachute into my rucksack, leaving a little corner of it hanging out over my shoulder so I could grab it fast in case I needed it. Traveling down to the river was easy; I just let myself fall forward and roll downhill. The grass cushioned my fall and slowed the speed of my roll. My head spun around and around, knocking all my senses out of whack. The little bamboo ends littering the field poked me in the ribs as I fell but I ignored them. "What the hell," I thought. "I'm dead already. What can possibly hurt me now?"

When I reached the bottom, I crawled ten feet through the undergrowth to the water's edge without bothering to check to see if the way was clear. I scooped up the river water in my hands and drank like a man who'd been lost in the desert. I don't know how long I lay there, but then I heard a clinking noise behind me. I turned and saw a villager with a fishnet coming my way. The bottom of the Laotian fishnets are weighted with lead or pieces of chain to make them easier to throw and quicker to sink. As the villager walked, the weights on his net clinked against each other and made the noise I had heard. He seemed to be walking right toward me and as I pressed myself tightly to the ground, his feet passed my face no more than an arm's length away. Even when he was out of sight, I was afraid to leave my hiding place. My filthy clothes and body blended with the jungle, camouflaging me well. The only giveaway was the stark white of my feet. I covered them with leaves and was half sitting, half lying, wondering what to do next, when I heard voices coming from the area where I'd first heard the fisherman's clinking net. My back was to the river and I had no place to run if I were seen. For a second I wondered if I should chance crawling into the heavier jungle, but it was too late. Seventeen pairs of legs filed past, one by one, so close that one of them nearly stepped on my hand. They were all armed and were Viet Cong, not villagers.

I waited for a while to be sure they were all past and there were no stragglers bringing up the rear, then began to follow them, my heart beating wildly. I was close enough that I could see them hunting for broken twigs, bent branches, and other signs. Every now and then one would find something and they would all gather around and talk about it before continuing upriver. I could tell they were excellent trackers because they were following my path exactly. Days had passed since I'd been here and my footprints were almost completely gone, but they were still able to retrace my route.

They sat down to rest. I squatted in the brush about a hundred yards away where I could see them. Suddenly, a voice called to me, "Dieter, Dieter!" It was Duane; I knew it was Duane. "Dieter, Dieter, give me your pants. My legs are cold." There was no doubt that it was Duane calling me. "But Duane's dead," I told myself. Then the voice was gone as suddenly as it had come.

The Viet Cong got up from their rest stop and continued their tracking up the bank. In time we came to the place where Duane and I had thrown the carbine away. From their voices I could tell they knew something had gone on here. They began searching the area. One of them yelled as he pulled the carbine out of the mud and raised it over his head. They resumed their careful tracking. They stayed together in a group and I kept them in sight at all times, except when they went around a bend in the trail. I had to be very careful at that point, as there was always the chance they would decide to take a rest just around the bend where I couldn't see them. Then I might unwittingly walk right into their arms. But I had lost all fear and it was merely strange and interesting to watch the trackers track me.

They stopped near where Duane and I had slept on the rocks and been sunburned. Some of them set about building a fire. Slowly and carefully I moved through the bush toward them until I was about a hundred feet away.

The Viet Cong herded together and prepared to ford the river. Even though my vision was blurred, I could see the individual men in the group quite clearly. A couple of them were wearing red jerseys. A few had blue ones, while the rest were dressed in loincloths. They started into the river and it amazed me that they could cross so easily in a swift current without being able to see the bottom. The last man to cross put out the fire. It began to rain and they put on plastic ponchos like the ones Phisit and Procet had had after the escape.

Suddenly one of them pointed straight across at me, but the rest of the group didn't act as if anything unusual was happening. Without warning, one of the Viet Cong slipped into the river and started toward me. I just lay there quietly in the bush and watched him come closer and closer. He didn't stop until he was only a few feet away, standing in the waist-deep water and searching for something under the surface. "It's a trick," I thought. "He knows I'm here hiding in the bush and he's got a rifle hidden under the water." The man had very dark hair and his arms were tattooed. I kept waiting for him to pull out a gun and blast me, but then he appeared with a fishing net held high above the water in his tattooed arms. I almost collapsed with relief as he turned around and started back to the other bank. I realized then that if he had really known I was there, he never would have had the guts to approach me alone; the Pathet Lao and Viet Cong always did their work in groups. Just the same, it had been an awfully close call.

As soon as the man with the fishnet joined the others, they started downriver on the other side. I waited until they were around the bend in the river and out of sight before I crawled out of my hiding place to the fire. The Viet Cong had left very little but I was able to find six kernels of rice, three small peppers, and a fish head. I also ate the leaf the fish head had been resting on because it, too, tasted fishy.

I thought about crossing the river but decided against it. I would be too exposed while I was in the water and anyone nearby could spot me easily. I crawled back to my first hiding place in the bush and tried to think of what I should do next, but I was so weak that I couldn't think. I was so terribly lonely and starved that it would have been a relief if the Viet Cong had found me and killed me.

I had been sitting there for maybe half an hour when three other Viet Cong passed by, heading upstream. I had counted all of the guerrillas and I couldn't figure out where these three had come from. They looked mean, and watching their straw-sheathed machetes beat rhythmically against their backsides brought to mind Duane's death. Without stopping to rest, the three also forded the river. They spent a few minutes squatting on the opposite bank, then walked on and disappeared around the bend.

A strange thought struck me. Only a few minutes earlier I had been wishing, hoping, for death. Now these three guerrillas had been an opportunity for me to make that wish come true, but something had held me back. What was holding me back—a plain animal instinct for survival? Or was it something else?

Now that it was nearly dark, I risked leaving my hiding place to cross the river. At first the current was manageable but then it quickened and swept me downstream. Slowly I made it to the bank and vomited—a spastic vomiting so painful that I blacked out.

The nightmare now began in earnest; constant hallucination was my whole reality. I couldn't distinguish what I saw from what I imagined. I was crawling on my hands and knees, too weak even to move my head from side to side. Duane haunted me all the time. "Dieter, Dieter," he complained. "My legs are cold, Dieter, my legs are cold." He kept hounding me until I thought I would go mad if he repeated that once more. Then the prison camp appeared before me and I was back at Hoi Het, shackled and sick. All the men from the camp were talking to me. Then they went away and Duane was after me again. From that point on he never really left me but was always nearby, at the edge of my dreaming. During the day he gave me directions about what I should do, but with the coming of night he cried constantly about his cold legs. Sometimes I would doze off, then wake up twenty yards from where I had fallen asleep with my clothes wrapped around my legs.

Above me the golden door opened again. Racing chariots dashed out, and I threw up my arms to protect myself from the sharp, trampling hooves. I kept passing out, collapsing, vomiting. I had no idea where I was going, but I pushed on. I was crawling in the water when I happened across some snails. I popped them whole into my mouth, ground them up, shells and all, and swallowed. No longer did I feel pain and I wasn't sure whether I was dead or alive. I knew the end was near and as I crawled I prayed, because that was all I could do. I rolled on my stomach and struggled to my knees, begging God to let me live. Then Duane was calling, crying about his chilled legs. I gave him my parachute material and told him to use it like a blanket. Hours later and some distance away, I came awake, only to find the parachute wound tightly around my own legs. Then my father began to call out to me.

I became increasingly aware of the moon bear's presence. I stopped and turned toward the spot where he was, about fifteen feet away, and he didn't growl or show any sign of fear. I was almost glad to see him because I felt less alone. "Lead me out of here, bear," I said to him. "Lead me out." But the bear just lay down and watched me closely, occasionally shaking his head in response. I began to wonder if God had sent the animal to guide me out or to protect me. Or did the bear know that I was nearly dead and was he just waiting for me to kick off?

I came to a bend in the river and around it was a huge cascading waterfall. "That's where I'm going. Maybe I'll roll into the river in the dark and drown." I found a little place, four feet square, near the waterfall, with the water churning and foaming below me. I fell asleep and Duane was standing next to me. Before I had only heard his voice but now I saw him, full-blown. He must have been angry about something because the sight of him scared me and I had no place to hide from him. The bear was nearby, standing guard.

When I awoke in the morning, I thought I was choking to death. My throat was clogged with a thick, viscous gunk, streaked with red and white. Apparently the crushed snail shells had sliced through the lining of my stomach and caused internal bleeding. I tried to sit up but I was wedged tightly between two rocks a few yards from where I'd fallen asleep the night before. I was naked. I found my clothes lying between me and a wall of rock; it took me an endless time to put them on before crawling away. I had no destination but had to keep moving. I was hungry, as always, but hunger didn't drive me on so much as some inexplicable outside force that kept hounding me and pushing me forward. I continued on, inch by inch. I didn't even watch out for people. All my caution was gone and all I did was crawl and pray. I wanted only to go home. "Please give me the strength to make it home. I want to see home before I die," I prayed in my mind. I barely had the strength to move my lips.

The river narrowed and high cliffs towered above me. I welcomed the shade they gave me from the hot, baking sun. But even with the coolness, what remained of my strength kept fading away. I wondered how much longer I could keep going. Sometimes I couldn't move an inch and would lie still and say to myself: "This is it. I can't go on. Not one more step." Then I began thinking about death by starvation. I had visions of the bear or some other wild animal biting off my leg while I was still alive and was too weak to fight off anything that attacked me. My only hope was to keep moving. And with that thought I would find a new bit of strength to pull myself back up on my knees and keep going.

I thought about Marina, about whether she was waiting for me. I wondered whether my mother in Germany would have to wait seven years before I was declared dead. I thought of all the people I had wronged in my life and I prayed to God to forgive my sins and let me live to make up for them.

A slip sent me tumbling into the shallow river. My head cracked against a boulder and I stayed afloat only with the help of my rucksack, which I had stuffed with pieces of bamboo about a week before to use as an emergency life preserver. I eased myself up onto the large, flat rock in the middle of the small stream and noticed the moon bear standing on his hind legs on the opposite bank.

Though only a few inches above the surface of the water, the top of the boulder was dry and smooth, a good place to dry out and rest. One of the nearby boulders was hollowed out into a shallow, bowl-shaped depression, about five feet across and three feet deep, and in the bowl was coiled a brilliantly colored snake. Without even stopping to see if the snake was poisonous, I got into the bowl, beat the snake with my rucksack, and snatched it up. It coiled around my hand and arm, and I took the head in one hand and the tail in the other, pulling the snake taut and biting it in half. My mouth tasted of salt, as both ends of the snake coiled and writhed about my hands. The long brown liver hung from the gash in its body, and I began to eat it and kept eating it until half the snake was gone. I spread out the remainder of the carcass on the rock to dry, then lay down to rest.

Barely had my head touched the cool stone when I heard the rumbling of an approaching truck. The oddness of the noise shocked my mind to attention. "That's no truck," I thought, "my God, that's a plane!" Instinctively I reached over my shoulder and pulled the white parachute from my rucksack but only had enough strength to make one wave, as a plane that looked like a World War II Corsair passed overhead in a nearly vertical bank. I was sure I was seeing things, that the sun was getting to me and that the plane was a figment of my imagination. I thought of crawling into the bush to get away from the sun, then heard the aircraft approach again. The sound of its engine grew louder as it came closer, but it was still hidden by the high ridges around me. Then, for a few seconds, I saw it swooping down the narrow canyon. I realized that it was a Spad, the same kind of plane in which I'd been shot down. I stood up and began to pray out loud to God to send the Spad back again, while the sound of the engine grew fainter and fainter. Tears streamed down my face as I continued to stare up from the canyon at the strip of sky above me. Then I heard the plane come back my way again. As it came closer I waved frantically. I took the parachute in my hands and teeth and tried to tear it into strips, with no success. I laid the chute on the flat boulder in a distress signal. I didn't watch the plane as it passed over, just concentrated on making the signal. I was trying to make an S.O.S. but couldn't remember which way the "S" went.

The plane came again and as he was pulling out, he dipped his wings in recognition. I asked myself whether it might merely be turbulence and not recognition. This was the first indication that the pilot possibly had seen me. Frantic hope filled me, and I jumped from one boulder to another, trying to lay out the S.O.S. I ripped off my tan pants, which I had been wearing under my other rags, and added them to the signal, then stood and waved my naked arms at the now empty sky until I collapsed to my knees. I closed my eyes and prayed for the Spad to come back again. Then I rolled onto my back and spread-eagled myself across the top of the boulder, staring straight into the blue sky above.

A second Spad was now circling at about 2,000 feet. I knew he must be sending a radio message. The first Spad couldn't send or receive because the mountains were in his way. I kept looking for the other Spad, the low-flying one, but all I could see was the higher one, dashing in and out of the billowing white clouds to the west.

Then fear took over, spiking me with anxiety. What if this was only a dream? What if I was making all of it up in my mind? I was so afraid they would go away. "It must be real," I shouted into the sky. "Please let it be real," I begged. "Come back, you guys," I pleaded. "Don't leave me here. Please, please, don't leave me!"

First I could hear them and then I saw them. One was flying very high, while the second chopper shot overhead and disappeared behind the opposite ridge, its huge blades snapping the air and its green body covering me with an enormous fleeting shadow. "Down here, down here!" I screamed at them as they disappeared.

A shot echoed out down the canyon and I knew it was the Viet Cong. They must have figured out where I was and now they were coming up the canyon after me. It was a race, a race between the choppers and the enemy, and the choppers didn't know about them. My heart pounded and I waved and yelled into the sky.

On the third pass, the lower one crossed the canyon a few hundred feet upriver, and then something exploded right next to me. "They're bombing me," I thought. I couldn't believe it. I began scrambling through the water and into the jungle, but stopped when I smelled the stiff odor of gasoline. As the biting smell went up my nose, I knew for sure now that I wasn't dreaming—that this was for real. They had dropped their external fuel tanks.

An enormous Jolly Green Giant helicopter maneuvered carefully down to a position above me until he was about two hundred feet overhead. He had a hard time because the narrow canyon afforded little clearance for the whirling blades. The wind from his blades was vicious. A tree-penetrator descended slowly from the chopper's side, weaving back and forth as it came down to me. I was back on the rock waiting for it, each second an eternity. I prayed to God to let me get clear before the Viet Cong came around the bend, and again I heard shots echo in the canyon. The penetrator swung in front of me like a pendulum, nearly knocking me into the water.

I felt woozy and distant. "Come on, grab on," I urged myself. Finally I wrapped myself around the penetrator and swung back and forth with it until it quieted down and hung somewhat steadily. I had to open a zipper to pull down a leg to sit on, but it wouldn't give. Frantically I fumbled with the thing as I was knocked back and forth by the great wind from the blades. The shooting was getting closer—too close—and the chopper's blades whipped the air around me as I fought with the zipper. It finally gave, but then the penetrator slipped away from me. I grabbed again, holding on to it desperately. I pulled down one of the penetrator's three arms and sat across it. As soon as I was on, I waved my arm to signal the chopper to haul me in.

The arm of the penetrator between my legs tugged and I began to rise. There was a steady pull on my almost nonexistent body and I closed my arms and prayed to God to let me hold on just this little bit longer. I opened my eyes once as I rose to the chopper and the jungle was lush and green below. I began to spin around and around and closed my eyes again, holding on with a death grip. I was still being reeled in, far below the chopper, as he began to move off.

When I opened my eyes again, a huge man was towering over me in the doorway of the helicopter. He took hold of me and dragged me inside. I grabbed his leg and hugged it, refusing to let go, afraid that he might go away. My body began to shake violently, and I collapsed on the floor, unable to move. Loud, mumbling sobs poured out of me. "God, I'm alive. Oh, my God, I'm alive. Thank you, thank you so much. I'm alive." I sobbed and sobbed and the world went fuzzy again.

EPILOGUE

I remember very little of the trip in the helicopter except for bits of things, like a few frames picked at random from a length of film. I must have finally let go of the man's leg who pulled me aboard. Someone ripped off my rags. I had no idea what he was doing, but then everything in the last few days had seemed mysterious and strange, so this was no different. I lay on the floor, mumbling and sobbing loudly, and I must have been saying my name. A redheaded pilot stuck his head around the bulkhead and gave me a big smile. I was told later that the men in the chopper had fed me some beans and pineapple juice which I devoured greedily. At one point someone lifted me up to look out and I could see endless rows of jungle ridges. I remember thinking to myself how lucky I was because Duane and I had fooled ourselves into thinking we would see the ocean after crossing the next large ridge, when actually we were really about eighty miles off.

We landed where people were running every which way. A man with a white shirt bombarded me with questions and a photographer's flashgun went off in my face. Within minutes I was carried to another, smaller helicopter, with a soldier standing guard at the machine gun in the open doorway.

Then I was in bed, in a hospital in Da Nang. The next few days passed quickly, a succession of real life and afterlife: transfusions, injections, tests, a bath, a shave, and many tears. I kept mumbling to be taken to my friends on the *Ranger*.

On my third or fourth day at Da Nang, someone came into

my room, picked me up, and raced with me out of the back door of the barracks-like hospital building. Bouncing around in the front seat of a truck, we sped over sand dunes, crossed a bridge, passed people, oxcarts, and bicycles. We stopped at the Da Nang airport. Someone wrapped me in a blanket and shoved me under a table, telling me not to make a sound. I had no idea what was happening.

Twenty minutes later I was in an S2F, a navy plane. The doctor sitting next to the metal basket in which I was lying lifted my head toward the window. The plane banked and there, just below us, was my ship, the carrier *Ranger*. My own buddies had kidnapped me from Da Nang. Suddenly I was so excited I couldn't wait to see everyone. "What will Norm say?" I wondered. "And Spook? Wow, now he won't be able to collect on that insurance!"

The tires of the S2F squealed in the old familiar way, and then the plane decelerated quickly, as it had picked up the wire across the carrier's deck. We taxied forward. The large elevator carried the aircraft down into the hangar deck of the ship.

The next few minutes were indescribable. There was a red carpet and thousands of men yelled and cheered. Friends hugged me and we cried. I was maneuvered down the steep steps, through the gangways, along the narrow corridors, and hands and arms reached out to me. They had a big cake for the celebration and everyone had a million questions. I was the happiest man on earth. They put me in the admiral's quarters where friends, doctors, and food kept me busy constantly. The only bad moments I had were at night. Sleep brought back the nightmares of captivity in the jungle and I would scream and fight my way out of the room. Guards were stationed at the doors to make sure I didn't do myself any harm.

I soon found out that my rescue was a sort of miraculous mixture of coincidence, luck, and God's intercession. To begin with, all the traveling Duane and I had done had taken us only a short way from Hoi Het. At one point, Duane and I had actually backtracked to an area a mile and a half from the prison, and the spot where I was picked up was only about five miles from the camp. We had wandered for about twenty-three days in the lap of the Viet Cong and somehow had managed to elude them. However, that bit of luck was nothing compared to the miraculous series of circumstances that led to my being spotted by the Spad. The pilot, Gene Deatrick, was a newcomer to Vietnam who had just been assigned a skipper at Pleiku Air Base. On the morning of July 20, 1966, while I was crawling about hallucinating madly, Gene was getting ready for an area familiarization flight. It was raining and no day to fly, but he insisted on flying anyway. After he got his Spad and fired her up, he lost the generator and had to abort his takeoff. Most pilots would have just said to hell with it because the flight was not scheduled anyway, but he insisted on going that day. Soon he was in the air in another aircraft, followed by his wingman, whose job it was to acquaint him with the country by pointing out prominent landmarks, gun emplacements, rivers, roads, and so on. Their course took them in my direction but there was no news at all of escaped prisoners, nor had either pilot heard about a burned-down village.

Soon the overcast sky fell behind and the sky turned blue and clear. The country was an unending succession of lush mountain ridges, each one a carbon copy of the one before it, separated only by deep and very narrow canyons. Occasionally Gene would call his wingman about some river, or village, or to point the way to the Mugia Pass, but for the most part they just flew and looked around. Acting on a sudden, unreasoned impulse, he banked to the right, calling out to his wingman that he was going in to explore one particular canyon which looked a little larger than the others nearby. He had flown perhaps twenty seconds when he changed his mind and decided to rejoin his wingman, and he rolled into a steep left bank.

Because the wings of a Spad are set into the fuselage right under the canopy, a pilot can see the ground directly beneath him only when he banks ninety degrees. When Gene was perhaps three seconds into this steep bank, and only during those few seconds, he saw a flash of something white on the ground, a thousand feet below. I was lying on a flat boulder and waving a parachute, but all Gene saw was that brief flash of white.

Most pilots would have dismissed the incident and never have given it another thought, but to Gene, so new to the game, it appeared to be someone shooting or perhaps some enemy coming down this canyon. He then realized that for the last half hour he had not seen a road, a village, or any sign of life, and he wondered what this strange thing was down below. He went back for another look but it took him a while to locate the canyon again because it looked just like all the others. This time he came in fast and low in a steep left bank. Now he saw the waving and this time the form of a man. He called out to his wingman, "Hey, there's some nut down there waving at me."

At that point, a seasoned pilot would have assumed that it was a trap to sucker a pilot into an ambush. Gene's wingman urged him on, telling him to forget it, but something made him stay. A radio call went out to Pleiku, saying they had spotted what could be a downed pilot. His home base checked around with the others and also with the carriers to see if they were missing anyone. The answer was "no" and they were told to disregard the sighting. No one even knew where Hoi Het was, much less that we had broken out, so the idea of an escaped POW didn't occur to anyone. Gene's curiosity and his strange feeling that he had stumbled onto something important kept him from leaving the area. Because of his rank, he was able to insist on staying and requested that choppers be sent out. He and his wingman moved some distance away so that their presence wouldn't give away my positon. After a long wait, two Jolly Green Giants arrived.

By some strange coincidence, the commander of the choppers was Skip Cowell, the same pilot who had been searching for me six months before, and whom I had seen overhead on the river the day I was captured. Skip naturally was worried about an ambush, so he made his first run over the canyon at high speed to draw enemy fire. Fortunately for me the Viet

Cong down the canyon didn't take a shot at him because if they had, he would have considered me bait and returned to home plate without so much as another look. Carefully, but without hesitation, Skip began to drop down into this narrow canyon in his giant helicopter. To make it lighter and to maneuver more easily, he dropped his two external fuel tanks, setting off the explosions I had thought were bombs. The fit was too tight for him to get any lower than two hundred feet from where they had lowered the tree-penetrator to me.

As the penetrator wobbled down, the helicopter crew got a good look at me. Because I weighed only ninety pounds and my clothes were nothing but filthy, tattered rags, they couldn't figure out who I was and even assumed I was probably a Laotian or Vietnamese. As I struggled with the tree-penetrator and they pulled me up toward the chopper, they kept their machine guns aimed at me, fearing that I was one of those fanatics who would sacrifice themselves to bag a helicopter at close range with a hand grenade. They were particularly nervous when I was really close to them. I probably saved my life when I unfolded only one of the penetrator legs and had to hang on for dear life, because if I had so much as made an enthusiastic wave toward the chopper, they probably would have blasted me out of the sky. As soon as I was near the door, the paramedics grabbed me, pulled me inside, and tore off my clothes to look for a hidden hand grenade or concealed weapon. Only when they saw the color of my skin and my beard did they realize I might be an American. I kept mumbling my name, but since I had been listed as missing six months before, they couldn't trace me and it was not until they got to Da Nang that they could positively identify me.

Since I was one of the first POWs to escape, the navy still had no established procedures for handling cases like mine, and they weren't sure what to do with me. From the *Ranger* I was sent to Guam, then to Travis Air Force Base in California, where I was reunited with Marina and my brother and his wife. I finally ended up at Balboa Naval Hospital in San Diego, under the care of a navy captain by the name of Allan Holmes, who was more like a father to me than a doctor, and who helped and guided me through my recovery.

I had a lot of recovering to do. I was so malnourished that if I hadn't been picked up when I was, I would have died that day or the next. My liver was in such bad shape that for months afterwards I couldn't drink that long-awaited beer. Two types of malaria, worms, fungus, and other infections slowed the initial recovery. When I was picked up I weighed only 90 pounds—70 pounds down from my normal 160—and was so weak I had to be carried to the john.

After I recovered, my life seemed an endless and frenetic progression of debriefings, newspaper reporters, relatives, and so on. Because of the presence of reporters and the press stories about me—some true but most false—Marina and I were unable to plan or even think about a peaceful wedding. Finally we were forced to elope to Reno. I had little time to indulge in the quiet pleasures of married life and was kept busy with a constant round of press conferences and speaking engagements, even an appearance before the Congress of the United States.

After a short training period as a jet pilot at Lemoore Naval Air Station near Fresno, and then another year with V.C.7 at Miramar Naval Air Station in San Diego, I was discharged from the navy in February 1968. I went to work with TWA, starting at the bottom as a flight engineer, based first in New York and then in San Francisco.

Marina and I gave each other our freedom after four years of marriage. She was a dedicated career woman, determined that nothing would stop her from becoming a professor of marine biology. As for me, I couldn't get used to the domestic routine of married life—buying furniture, having newspapers delivered, and all the "don'ts" that come with marriage—so we parted as good friends.

When the airlines fell on hard times, I was furloughed twice. I took advantage of the time and my freedom as a bachelor to make a trip around the world—by motorcycle, hitchhiking, and on foot. I visited Vientienne in Laos, as well as Thailand, Borneo, India, and Nepal, and also made a trip down the Amazon.

I had heard that Phisit had separated from the group, was recaptured and severely beaten. He happened to be in a camp that was overrun by Laotian Royalist troops. Supposedly he is today somewhere in Thailand.

Duane was promoted posthumously to captain in the U.S. Air Force on July 21, 1966, and awarded the Distinguished Flying Cross.

Gene, Procet, Y.C., and Thani have never been heard of again. The story is over.

Now I live in Sausalito, across the Golden Gate from San Francisco.

One thought, however, is with me always—that I am alive and a free man!

About the author

Dieter Dengler was born in Germany in 1938 and emigrated to the United States in 1957. He enlisted in the U.S. Air Force and, after his discharge in 1961, enrolled at San Francisco City College. He later transferred to San Mateo Junior College where he studied aeronautics and was awarded the 1962 Air Youth Award which is given to outstanding students in that field.

In 1963 he was accepted for naval flight training and a year later was commissioned an ensign. In December of 1965 his squadron embarked aboard the aircraft carrier U.S.S. *Ranger*, and he was soon flying missions over North Vietnam.

In February of 1966 he was shot down over Laos and captured by the Communist Pathet Lao. His unprecedented escape five months later made the front pages of newspapers across the country and around the world and prompted articles in *Time* magazine, *The Saturday Evening Post*, and other publications.

Lieutenant Dengler received the U.S. Navy's highest award, the Navy Cross, as well as the Distinguished Flying Cross, Air Medal, and Purple Heart. After completing his tour of duty in the navy, he joined Trans World Airlines as a pilot and is presently based in San Francisco.